DESERTS

JOURNEYING THROUGH THE WILDERNESS
TO EXPERIENCE GOD'S PROVISION

KAT ARMSTRONG

NavPress

Published in alliance with Tyndale House Publishers

NavPress.com

I'm convinced that the Bible is somehow powerfully simple and beautifully complex. Like a diamond viewed from different angles, Scripture continually confronts my heart in fresh ways. This Bible-study series offers insightful perspectives and gives its participants a refreshing opportunity to admire the character of God and be transformed by the truth of his Word. Our souls need to meander through the minutiae and metanarrative of the Bible, and the **Storyline Bible Studies** help us do both.

KYLE IDLEMAN, senior pastor of Southeast Christian Church and bestselling author of *Not a Fan* and *One at a Time*

If you are longing for a breath of fresh air in your spiritual life, this study is for you. Kat Armstrong brings to life both familiar and less familiar Bible stories in such an engaging way that you can't help but see how the God of the past is also working and moving in your present. Through the captivating truths revealed in this series, you will discover more about God's faithfulness, be equipped to move past fear and disappointment, and be empowered to be who you were created to be. If your faith has felt mundane or routine, these words will be a refreshing balm to your soul and a guide to go deeper in your relationship with God.

HOSANNA WONG, international speaker and bestselling author of *How (Not) to Save the World: The Truth about Revealing God's Love to the People Right Next to You*

We are watching a new wave of Bible studies that care about the Bible's big story, from Genesis to Revelation; that plunge Bible readers into the depths of human despair and show them the glories of the Kingdom God plans for creation; and that invite readers to participate in that story in all its dimensions—in the mountains and the valleys. Anyone who ponders these Bible studies will come to terms not only with the storyline of the Bible but also with where each of us fits in God's grand narrative. I heartily commend Kat's **Storyline Bible Studies**.

REV. CANON DR. SCOT McKNIGHT, New Testament scholar, author, professor, and host of the *Kingdom Roots* podcast

Kat Armstrong is an able trail guide with contagious enthusiasm! In this series, she'll take you hiking through Scripture to experience mountains and valleys, sticks and stones, sinners and saints. If you are relatively new to the Bible or are struggling to see how it all fits together, your trek with Kat will be well worth it. You might even decide that hiking through the Bible is your new hobby.

CARMEN JOY IMES, associate professor of Old Testament at Biola University and author of *Bearing God's Name: Why Sinai Still Matters*

Kat Armstrong takes you into the heart of Scripture so that Scripture can grow in your heart. The **Storyline Bible Studies** have everything: the overarching story of God's redemption, the individual biblical story's historical context, and the text's interpretation that connects with today's realities. Armstrong asks insightful questions that make the Bible come alive and draws authentically on her own faith journey so that readers might deepen their relationship with Jesus. Beautifully written and accessible, the **Storyline Bible Studies** are a wonderful resource for individual or group study.

LYNN H. COHICK, PhD, distinguished professor of New Testament and director of Houston Theological Seminary at Houston Christian University

Christians affirm that the Bible is God's Word and provides God's life-giving instruction and encouragement. But what good is such an authoritative and valuable text if God's people don't engage it to find the help the Scriptures provide? Here's where Kat Armstrong's studies shine. In each volume, she presents Bible study as a journey through Scripture that can be transformational. In the process, she enables readers to see the overarching storyline of the Bible and to find their place in that story. In addition, Armstrong reinforces the essential steps that make Bible study life-giving for people seeking to grow in their faith. Whether for individuals, for small groups, or as part of a church curriculum, these studies are ideally suited to draw students into a fresh and invigorating engagement with God's Word.

WILLIAM W. KLEIN, PhD, professor emeritus of New Testament interpretation and author of *Handbook for Personal Bible Study: Enriching Your Experience with God's Word*

Kat has done two things that I love. She's taken something that is familiar and presented it in a fresh way that is understandable by all, balancing the profound with accessibility. And her trustworthy and constant approach to Bible study equips the participant to emerge from this study with the ability to keep studying and growing more.

MARTY SOLOMON, creator and executive producer of *The BEMA Podcast*

You are in for an adventure. In this series, Kat pulls back the curtain to reveal how intentionally God has woven together seemingly disconnected moments in the collective Bible story. Her delivery is both brilliant and approachable. She will invite you to be a curious sleuth as you navigate familiar passages of Scripture, discovering things you'd never seen before. I promise you will never read the living Word the same again.

JENN JETT BARRETT, founder and visionary of The Well Summit

Kat has done it again! The same wisdom, depth, humility, and authenticity that we have come to expect from her previous work is on full display here in her new **Storyline Bible Study** series. Kat is the perfect guide through these important themes and through the story of Scripture: gentle and generous on the one hand, capable and clear on the other. She is a gifted communicator and teacher of God's Word. The format of these studies is helpful too— perfect pacing, just the right amount of new information at each turn, with plenty of space for writing and prayerful reflection as you go and some great resources for further study. I love learning from Kat, and I'm sure you will too. Grab a few friends from your church or neighborhood and dig into these incredible resources together to find your imagination awakened and your faith strengthened.

DAN LOWERY, president of Pillar Seminary

Kat Armstrong possesses something I deeply admire: a sincere and abiding respect for the Bible. Her tenaciousness to know more about her beloved Christ, her commitment to truth telling, and her desire to dig until she mines the deepest gold for her Bible-study readers makes her one of my favorite Bible teachers. I find few that match her scriptural attentiveness and even fewer that embody her humble spirit. This project is stunning, like the rest of her work.

LISA WHITTLE, bestselling author of *Jesus over Everything: Uncomplicating the Daily Struggle to Put Jesus First*, Bible teacher, and podcast host

For my dad, Ronald K. Obenhaus.
I think you would have loved this.

Contents

A Message from Kat

OUR FAMILY'S going through some stuff.

Nothing life-threatening, but lots of our dreams feel stuck in a wasteland. Our lives don't resemble what we imagined. And plans? What plans? At this point, those are irrelevant. We've had to let go so often we've almost forgotten what it's like to be held.

As eager as I am to be done with this season of disappointment, my faith reminds me that disappointment can do good and holy work, drawing us all closer to Christ. Even though I want to count this stretch of badlands a loss, I can't—and won't—because that's not how God's terrain works. This wandering part of my journey has value. And so does yours. God will eventually reroute our dead ends to a way through.

I'm ready to be through confusion so that I can arrive at clarity. I know I'll look back with hindsight and be thankful that the Lord carried me through what felt like a maze of letdowns. But for now, I'm still stuck in no-man's-land. As I wait on the Lord to direct my steps and bring clarity to my family, I've found myself exploring the deserts of Scripture.

In this Bible study, you're going to discover that deserts in the Bible are more than geographical locations. Deserts represent the lonely and sometimes vast lostness we sense when our lives take unplanned detours. The Bible is full of stories of people making harrowing journeys through deserts—Hagar, Joseph, Moses, and Jesus, to name a few. And every desert we visit in our study together will create a storyline threaded throughout Scripture: God is faithful to make a way when there is none.

God Almighty meets you in your desert moments. The deserts in your life do not separate you from God's presence. In fact, your wilderness wanderings might amplify God's presence in your life if you learn to look for his loving attention to your deepest needs.

Just when we think we are going to die in the desert, the Lord supplies what we need to get to the other side. You see, your wilderness wanderings are a way to God's protection, to restoration, to a deep sense of belonging, to new ministry opportunities, and to an abundance that will wow you with God's love.

Love,

Kat

The LORD will comfort Zion;
 he will comfort all her waste places,
and will make her wilderness like Eden,
 her desert like the garden of the LORD;
joy and gladness will be found in her,
 thanksgiving and the voice of song.

ISAIAH 51:3

The Storyline of Scripture

YOUR DECISION TO STUDY THE BIBLE for the next few weeks is no accident—God has brought you here, to this moment. And I don't want to take it for granted. Here, at the beginning, I want to invite you into the most important step you can take, the one that brings the whole of the Bible alive in extraordinary ways: a relationship with Jesus.

The Bible is a collection of divinely inspired manuscripts written over fifteen hundred years by at least forty different authors. Together, the manuscripts make up tens of thousands of verses, sixty-six books, and two testaments. Point being: It's a lot of content.

But the Bible is really just one big story: God's story of redemption. From Genesis to Revelation the Bible includes narratives, songs, poems, wisdom literature, letters, and even apocalyptic prophecies. Yet everything we read in God's Word helps us understand God's love and his plan to be in a relationship with us.

If you hear nothing else, hear this: God loves you.

It's easy to get lost in the vast amount of information in the Bible, so we're going to explore the storyline of Scripture in four parts. And as you locate your experience in the story of the Bible, I hope the story of redemption becomes your own.

PART 1: GOD MADE SOMETHING GOOD.

The big story—God's story of redemption—started in a garden. When God launched his project for humanity, he purposed all of us—his image bearers—to flourish and co-create with him. In the beginning there was peace, beauty, order, and abundant life. The soil was good. Life was good. We rarely hear this part of our story, but it doesn't make it less true. God created something good—and that includes you.

PART 2: WE MESSED IT UP.

If you've ever thought, *This isn't how it's supposed to be,* you're right. It's not. We messed up God's good world. Do you ever feel like you've won gold medals in messing things up? Me too. All humanity shares in that brokenness. We are imperfect. The people we love are imperfect. Our systems are jacked, and our world is broken. And that's on us. We made the mess, and we literally can't help ourselves. We need to be rescued from our circumstances, the systems in which we live, and ourselves.

PART 3: JESUS MAKES IT RIGHT.

The good news is that God can clean up all our messes, and he does so through the life, death, and resurrection of Jesus Christ. No one denies that Jesus lived and died. That's just history. It's the empty tomb and the hundreds of eyewitnesses who saw Jesus after his death that make us scratch our heads. Because science can only prove something that is repeatable, we are dependent upon the eyewitness testimonies of Jesus' resurrection for this once-in-history moment. If Jesus rose from the dead—and I believe he did—Jesus is exactly who he said he was, and he accomplished exactly what had been predicted for thousands of years. He restored us. Jesus made *it*, all of it, right. He can forgive your sins and connect you to the holy God through his life, death, and resurrection.

PART 4: ONE DAY, GOD WILL MAKE ALL THINGS NEW.

The best news is that this is not as good as it gets. A day is coming when Christ will return. He's coming back to re-create our world: a place with no tears, no pain, no suffering, no brokenness, no helplessness—just love. God will make all things new. In the meantime, God invites you to step into his storyline, to join him in his work of restoring all things. Rescued restorers live with purpose and on mission: not a life devoid of hardship, but one filled with enduring hope.

RESPONDING TO GOD'S STORYLINE

If the storyline of Scripture feels like a lightbulb turning on in your soul, that, my friend, is the one true, living God, who eternally exists as Father, Son, and Holy Spirit. God is inviting you into a relationship with him to have your sins forgiven and secure a place in his presence forever. When you locate your story within God's story of redemption, you begin a lifelong relationship with God that brings meaning, hope, and restoration to your life.

Take a moment now to begin a relationship with Christ:

God, I believe the story of the Bible, that Jesus is Lord and you raised him from the dead to forgive my sins and make our relationship possible. Your storyline is now my story. I want to learn how to love you and share your love with others. Amen.

If you confess with your lips that Jesus is Lord and believe in your heart that God raised him from the dead, you will be saved.

ROMANS 10:9

How to Use This Bible Study

THE **STORYLINE BIBLE STUDIES** are versatile and can be used for

+ individual study (self-paced),
+ small groups (five- or ten-lesson curriculum), or
+ church ministry (semester-long curriculum).

INDIVIDUAL STUDY

Each lesson in the *Deserts* Bible study is divided into four fifteen- to twenty-minute parts (sixty to eighty minutes of individual study time per lesson). You can work through the material one part at a time over a few different days or all in one sitting. Either way, this study will be like anything good in your life: What you put in, you get out. Each of the four parts of each lesson will help you practice Bible-study methods.

SMALL GROUPS

Working through the *Deserts* Bible study with a group could be a catalyst for life change. Although the Holy Spirit can teach you truth when you read the Bible on your own, I want to encourage you to gather a small group together to work through this study for these reasons:

+ God himself is in communion as one essence and three persons: Father, Son, and Holy Spirit.
+ Interconnected, interdependent relationships are hallmarks of the Christian faith life.
+ When we collaborate with each other in Bible study, we have access to the viewpoints of our brothers and sisters in Christ, which enrich our understanding of the truth.

For this Bible study, every small-group member will need a copy of the *Deserts* study guide. In addition, I've created a free downloadable small-group guide that includes

+ discussion questions for each lesson,
+ Scripture readings, and
+ prayer prompts.

Whether you've been a discussion leader for decades or just volunteered to lead a group for the first time, you'll find the resources you need to create a loving atmosphere for men and women to grow in Christlikeness. You can download the small-group guide using this QR code.

CHURCH MINISTRY

Church and ministry leaders: Your work is sacred. I know that planning and leading through a semester of ministry can be both challenging and rewarding. That's why every **Storyline Bible Study** is written so that you can build modular semesters of ministry. The *Deserts* Bible study is designed to complement the

Gardens Bible study. Together, *Gardens* and *Deserts* can support a whole semester of ministry seamlessly, inviting the people you lead into God's Word and making your life simpler.

To further equip church and ministry leaders, I've created *The Leader's Guide*, a free digital resource. You can download *The Leader's Guide* using this QR code.

The Leader's Guide offers these resources:

+ a sample ministry calendar for a ten-plus-lesson semester of ministry,
+ small-group discussion questions for each lesson,
+ Scripture readings for each lesson,
+ prayer prompts for each lesson,
+ five teaching topics for messages that could be taught in large-group settings, and
+ resources for deeper study.

SPECIAL FEATURES

However you decide to utilize the *Deserts* Bible study, whether for individual, self-paced devotional time; as a small-group curriculum; or for semester-long church ministry, you'll notice several stand-out features unique to the **Storyline Bible Studies:**

+ gospel presentation at the beginning of each Bible study;
+ full Scripture passages included in the study so that you can mark up the text and keep your notes in one place;
+ insights from diverse scholars, authors, and Bible teachers;
+ an emphasis on close readings of large portions of Scripture;
+ following one theme instead of focusing on one verse or passage;
+ Christological narrative theology without a lot of church-y words; and
+ retrospective or imaginative readings of the Bible to help Christians follow the storyline of Scripture.

You may have studied the Bible by book, topic, or passage before; all those approaches are enriching ways to read the Word of God. The **Storyline Bible Studies** follow a literary thread to deepen your appreciation for God's master plan of redemption and develop your skill in connecting the Old Testament to the New.

THE DESERTS STORYLINE

WHEN I PICTURE A DESERT, my mind goes to movie series like *Indiana Jones*, *Star Wars*, *The Mummy*, and *Dune*—all of which have scenes where the main character is vulnerable and isolated in a place they can't survive. Deserts, no thank you.

And yet somehow, in each of those stories, deserts don't lead to death. Instead, the desert becomes the place where the hero faces a challenge and overcomes, or at least survives to fight another day.

God does something similar with desert settings in the Bible, repurposing the winding journey through unsurvivable lands as a backdrop for stories about his protection, provision, and providence. The *Deserts* Bible study will show us God's intentionality: that truths about who God is and what he does are woven into storylines through these geographical locations in Scripture.

As you may have seen through other **Storyline Bible Studies**, places didn't just matter in the ancient world—they had meaning. Locations are not solely pins on a map; they are loaded with historical significance and serve as connection points in God's unified story of redemption from the Old Testament to the New.

As you study deserts in Scripture, you're going to notice that the same God who met Hagar and Joseph in the desert—during their most desperate times—led Moses, the Israelites, and Jesus into deserts too. The desert is not a place of God's punishment but rather a pathway forward to better things. Although it rarely feels that way at the time.

This Bible study will help you discover an all-important truth: God meets your needs in your metaphorical deserts. Maybe that's what you need to hear more than anything else right now. God has not abandoned you to your circumstances. Like he has done with everyone else he's led through the desert, he will accompany you faithfully to the other side of this part of your journey.

In *Deserts*, we're going to explore

+ *Genesis 16, 21*: the Deserts of Shur and Beersheba, where Hagar met and named God;
+ *Genesis 37, 45, 50*: the Desert of Dothan, where Joseph got thrown into a pit;
+ *Numbers 11, 14*: the Desert of Sinai, where Moses and the Israelites wandered in the wilderness;
+ *Matthew 3–4*: the Desert of Judea, where Jesus was tested; and
+ *Matthew 14, 15*: the Deserts of Ministry, where Jesus fed the multitudes.

We're going to do this by looking at each desert story through four different lenses:

+ **PART 1: CONTEXT.** Do you ever feel dropped into a Bible story disoriented? Part 1 will introduce you to the desert you're going to study and help you study its story in its scriptural context. Getting your bearings before you read will enable you to answer the question *What am I about to read?*

✦ **PART 2: SEEING.** Do you ever read on autopilot? I do too. Sometimes I finish reading without a clue as to what just happened. A better way to read the Bible is to practice thoughtful, close reading of Scripture to absorb the message God is offering to us. That's why part 2 includes close Scripture reading and observation questions to empower you to answer the question *What is the story saying?*

✦ **PART 3: UNDERSTANDING.** If you've ever scratched your head after reading your Bible, part 3 will give you the tools to understand the author's intended meaning both for the original audience and for you. Plus you'll practice connecting the Old and New Testaments to get a fuller picture of God's unchanging grace. Part 3 will enable you to answer the question *What does it mean?*

✦ **PART 4: RESPONDING.** The purpose of Bible study is to help you become more Christlike; that's why part 4 will include journaling space for your reflection on and responses to the content and a blank checklist for actionable next steps. You'll be able to process what you're learning so that you can live out the concepts and pursue Christlikeness. Part 4 will enable you to answer the questions *What truths is this passage teaching?* and *How do I apply this to my life?*

One of my prayers for you, as a curious Bible reader, is that our journey through this study will help you cultivate a biblical imagination so that you're able to make connections throughout the whole storyline of the Bible. In each lesson, I'll do my best to include a few verses from different places in the Bible that are connected to our desert stories. In the course of this study, we'll see the way God shows up in deserts throughout his Word—and get a glimpse of how he might show up in our lives today.

God's Word is so wonderful, I hardly know how to contain my excitement. Feel free to geek out with me; let your geek flag fly high, my friends. When we can see how interrelated all the parts of Scripture are to each other, we'll find our affection for God stirred as we see his artistic brilliance unfold.

GOING THROUGH REJECTION TO GET TO PROTECTION

THE DESERTS OF SHUR AND BEERSHEBA: WHERE HAGAR MEETS AND NAMES GOD

SCRIPTURE: GENESIS 16, 21

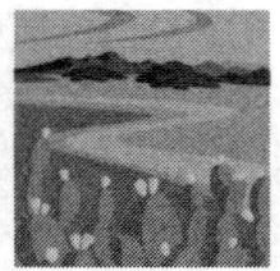

CONTEXT

Before you begin your study, we will start with the context of the story we are about to read together: the setting, both cultural and historical; the people involved; and where our passage fits in the larger setting of Scripture. All these things help us make sense of what we're reading. Understanding the context of a Bible story is fundamental to reading Scripture well. Getting your bearings before you read will enable you to answer the question *What am I about to read?*

WHEN YOU'RE A WRITER, rejection comes with the territory. I remember the sting of my first rejection email from a literary agent. In only a few minutes, the agent had reviewed and summarily dismissed a proposal I'd worked on for months, in which I'd filleted my heart and quantified every possible metric that might have made me a worthy investment to publishers. You think your days of getting picked for red rover are over when you reach adulthood—and then you start a job search, or throw your hat in for a promotion, or submit your first book proposal. That's when you remember how terrifying it is to raise your hand and say, "Pick me."

The agent told me that no one would want to read my book idea, a topic that was dear to my heart and close to my personal experience. He did mention, though, that I had a good personality. It wasn't me; it was my content.

After signing my first book contract, with a different agent, and turning in a completed manuscript for *No More Holding Back*, I received legal notice from the publisher that my manuscript was being rejected. I had thirty days to rewrite the entire book, resubmit it, and pray that they wanted to move forward. By God's grace, the title was published. But in those thirty days my prayer life went from inviting God to bless the work of my hands to begging God to steady my trembling fingers as I typed sixty thousand new words.

Maybe your story is not publishing books and Bible studies, but you know good and well how fast we recoil after being dismissed, refused, or ignored. Whether you've put yourself out there on a dating app, in a new small group, or at work, you've experienced being turned down. It cuts deep.

The first two deserts we are going to visit in our studies together will be the Desert of Shur and the Desert of Beersheba. For Hagar, an enslaved woman on the run, both locations represented rejection. Sadly, the rejection Hagar experienced in these two deserts is much more severe than anything I've described. Her abuse is in a category all its own.

Hagar's story is set in a place where many people get lost and die of thirst. But not Hagar or her son. God brought them through the most severe form of rejection to get them to a place of protection.

Reading Hagar's story without background knowledge of Ancient Near Eastern culture would be like wearing flip-flops on a hike through the desert. You'd get gritty sand stuck between your toes, making for a terribly painful journey. You and I need to familiarize ourselves with Ancient Near Eastern legal traditions, such as the Code of Hammurabi and the Lipit-Ishtar Code, on three key elements in Hagar's story: slavery, surrogacy, and barrenness.

Slavery in the Bible

+ Although slavery in the Old Testament is not the same as the chattel slavery of the United States, humans owning other humans for any reason was not God's design for our world.

+ The Exodus, the freeing of the Hebrew slaves from the Egyptian pharaoh, is the defining salvific event in the Old Testament. It helps define who God is and what he does. He is the God who frees and saves slaves.[1]

+ The laws God gave his people to govern their behavior included instructions to set all Hebrew slaves free every fifty years, during the Year of Jubilee (Leviticus 25:8-10). Effectively, God designed a way to abolish slavery . . . over and over and over.

Surrogacy in the Ancient Near East

+ Female slaves "were considered both property and legal extensions of their mistress. As a result it would be possible for Sarai to have Hagar perform a variety of household tasks as well as to use her as a surrogate for her own barren womb."[2]

+ "Concubines did not have the full status of wives but were girls who came to the marriage with no dowry and whose role included childbearing. As a result concubinage would not be viewed as polygamy."[3]

+ "Surrogate mothers appear only in the ancestral narratives: Hagar and the two maidservants of Rachel and Leah (Gen 30). There is no contract mentioned here, since these women were all legal extensions of their mistress and any children they bore could be designated as the children of their mistress."[4]

+ "Women in the ancient world obtained honor through marriage and children. Although Hagar was a servant, the fact that she had conceived a child and Sarai had not gave her cause to hold her mistress in contempt. Sarai's reaction in abusing Hagar may be based on both jealousy and class difference."[5]

Barrenness in the Ancient Near East

+ "Failure to produce an heir was a major calamity for a family in the ancient world because it meant a disruption in the generational inheritance pattern and left no one to care for the couple in their old age."[6]

+ "Legal remedies were developed which allowed a man whose wife had failed to provide him with a son to impregnate a slave girl (Code of Hammurabi; Nuzi texts) or a prostitute (Lipit-Ishtar Code). The children from this relationship could then be acknowledged by the father as his heirs (Code of Hammurabi)."[7]

God could have easily omitted this story from the canon of Scripture, but instead, he chose to expose the wrongdoings of some of the original faith family. Although I prefer to skip over stories in the Bible like Hagar's, I am also comforted that our righteous God, the God of justice and mercy, intentionally gives Hagar's exploitation a place in his Word. In a way only God can, he simultaneously gives voice to Hagar's plight, tells on Sarai and Abram, teaches us how to avoid their mistakes, and ensures we know that he can be trusted to protect us.

Only God could author a literary masterpiece thousands of years old set in a totally different culture with ancient characters and settings we can hardly pronounce while also telling true stories we can all relate to for all time.

God wants us to move on from rejection and into his protection, just like Hagar.

This is not to say God wants or wills you to go through rejection. God is good. He has good plans for you, plans to prosper and not to harm you (Jeremiah 29:11). He may allow each of us to experience the consequences of our own sin or the sin of others, but we can be confident in God's character: He is always redeeming our stories. God is a protecting God. Give him long enough, and you'll see that he's working all things out for your good. Even through rejection.

You're about to read everything we know about Hagar. It's a story about God meeting us in our most painful moments of life. About how near he is to us when we've been excluded, belittled, and victimized. And it's also a story about making it through mistreatment to protection.

Susan Niditch, "Genesis," in *Women's Bible Commentary*

1. **PERSONAL CONTEXT:** What is going on in your life right now that might impact how you understand Hagar's story in the Deserts of Shur and Beersheba? What do you hope to learn from this lesson?

2. **SPIRITUAL CONTEXT:** If you've never studied deserts in the Bible or Hagar's story before, what piques your curiosity? If you've studied these topics before, what impressions and insights do you recall?

3. **BIBLICAL CONTEXT:** What questions come to mind as you read about the context of Hagar's story? What questions do you wish you could have answered before studying this part of Scripture?

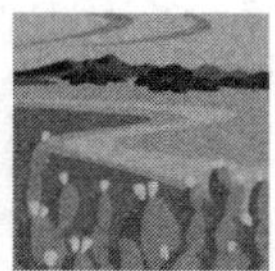

SEEING

Seeing the text is vital if we want the heart of the Scripture passage to sink in. We read slowly and intentionally through the text with the context in mind. As we practice close, thoughtful reading of Scripture, we pick up on phrases, implications, and meanings we might otherwise have missed. Part 2 includes close Scripture reading and observation questions to empower you to answer the question *What is the story saying?*

MY ELEVEN-YEAR-OLD SON, Caleb, loves Marvel movies—particularly the origin stories of superheroes like Spider-Man and Iron Man. Because he knows their backstories, Caleb interprets their present-day behaviors through the lens of their pasts. Someone's origin story can explain a lot.

Abraham and Sarah's origin story starts long before either of them is born—with the first humans, Adam and Eve, who chose to reject God's instructions and invitation to help the world flourish (Genesis 1–3). After Adam and Eve were exiled from the Garden of Eden, everything spiraled further away from God's good plan for humanity. One of Adam and Eve's sons murdered another. Human beings built a tower to once again proclaim to God that they didn't need him. Evil abounded. That's when God cleaned house with a great flood. Then he invited a new couple to join him in bringing about his intention for our world: to bless everyone (Genesis 12).

Enter Abraham and Sarah. Or, since we're in their origin story, we'll use their original names: Abram and Sarai. These two people were called by God to launch a movement. Physically, they were asked by God to leave their home. Spiritually, they were asked to bring a blessing to the whole world through their faith in God. God promised to make them into a great nation, which was another way of saying that he was going to give them children who would have children . . . until their family tree had too many branches to count.

The problem was that Sarai and Abram struggled with infertility. Unable to conceive, the couple resorted to shameful cultural practices that exposed their lack of faith in God.

1. Read Genesis 16:1–6. Underline any location markers described in the story.

16 Now Sarai, Abram's wife, bore him no children. She had an Egyptian slave-girl whose name was Hagar, ² and Sarai said to Abram, "You see that the LORD has prevented me from bearing children; go in to my slave-girl; it may be that I shall obtain children by her." And Abram listened to the voice of Sarai. ³ So, after Abram had lived ten years in the land of Canaan, Sarai, Abram's wife, took Hagar the Egyptian, her slave-girl, and gave her to her husband Abram as a wife. ⁴ He went in to Hagar, and she conceived; and when she saw that she had conceived, she looked with contempt on her mistress. ⁵ Then Sarai said to Abram, "May the wrong done to me be on you! I gave my slave-girl to your embrace, and when she saw that she had conceived, she looked on me with contempt. May the LORD judge between you and me!" ⁶ But Abram said to Sarai, "Your slave-girl is in your power; do to her as you please." Then Sarai dealt harshly with her, and she ran away from her.

GENESIS 16:1–6

2. **How does the Bible describe the problem Sarai and Abram were facing? What was Sarai's proposed solution?**

3. **Read Genesis 12:10-20 for more information on Sarai's backstory and then answer the questions that follow.**

10 Now there was a famine in the land. So Abram went down to Egypt to reside there as an alien, for the famine was severe in the land. 11 When he was about to enter Egypt, he said to his wife Sarai, "I know well that you are a woman beautiful in appearance; 12 and when the Egyptians see you, they will say, 'This is his wife'; then they will kill me, but they will let you live. 13 Say you are my sister, so that it may go well with me because of you, and that my life may be spared on your account." 14 When Abram entered Egypt the Egyptians saw that the woman was very beautiful. 15 When the officials of Pharaoh saw her, they praised her to Pharaoh. And the woman was taken into Pharaoh's house. 16 And for her sake he dealt well with Abram; and he had sheep, oxen, male donkeys, male and female slaves, female donkeys, and camels.

17 But the LORD afflicted Pharaoh and his house with great plagues because of Sarai, Abram's wife. 18 So Pharaoh called Abram, and said, "What is this you have done to me? Why did you not tell me that she was your wife? 19 Why did you say, 'She is my sister,' so that I took her for my wife? Now then, here is your wife, take her, and be gone." 20 And Pharaoh gave his men orders concerning him; and they set him on the way, with his wife and all that he had.

GENESIS 12:10-20

a. What happened to Sarai?

b. What was Abram's role in the story?

c. What did Abram and Sarai take with them when they left Egypt?

d. How do you think this experience would have impacted Sarai's and Abram's relationships with each other and with God?

As you process the harshness with which Sarai treated Hagar, I want you to consider that Sarai had experienced similar treatment from Abram in Egypt. In each case, a woman was seen as disposable property. A massive status and power gap existed between Abram and Sarai, just as it did between Sarai and Hagar. While in Egypt, Abram schemed to save his life at Sarai's expense. But in the story of Sarai and Hagar, Sarai is the one who's scheming to save her future at Hagar's expense.

When Sarai has the power to treat Hagar with mercy, she doesn't. She lords her status over Hagar without any empathy or understanding. Abram is no better. He is complicit in Hagar's abuse; he has the most power in the household, but he does not protest Sarai's treatment of Hagar and instead turns a blind eye.

While Sarai's backstory contains echoes of Hagar's experience, the two women couldn't be more different. The only thing Sarai and Hagar have in common is Abram.

DIFFERENCES BETWEEN SARAI AND HAGAR

Sarai	Hagar
Hebrew	Egyptian
wife	concubine/surrogate
rich	poor
free	enslaved
old	young
infertile	fertile

4. Read Genesis 16:7–16. Circle any mentions of the wilderness.

> ⁷ The angel of the LORD found her by a spring of water in the wilderness, the spring on the way to Shur. ⁸ And he said, "Hagar, slave-girl of Sarai, where have you come from and where are you going?" She said, "I am running away from my mistress Sarai." ⁹ The angel of the LORD said to her, "Return to your mistress, and submit to her." ¹⁰ The angel of the LORD also said to her, "I will so greatly multiply your offspring that they cannot be counted for multitude." ¹¹ And the angel of the LORD said to her,

"Now you have conceived and shall bear a son;
    you shall call him Ishmael,
    for the Lord has given heed to your affliction.
12 He shall be a wild ass of a man,
with his hand against everyone,
    and everyone's hand against him;
and he shall live at odds with all his kin."

13 So she named the Lord who spoke to her, "You are El-roi"; for she said, "Have I really seen God and remained alive after seeing him?" 14 Therefore the well was called Beer-lahai-roi; it lies between Kadesh and Bered.

15 Hagar bore Abram a son; and Abram named his son, whom Hagar bore, Ishmael. 16 Abram was eighty-six years old when Hagar bore him Ishmael.

GENESIS 16:7-16

5. How bad would your life have to be to run away from your home and family?

6. Write out Genesis 16:7 below:

For those of us who know the profound disorientation of being or feeling lost, God's activity in Hagar's life is all the more comforting.

God found her.

He will find us.

Hagar was discarded, disgraced, and displaced. *But God.* He came near to her in her time of greatest need. You and I can trust that he will show up for us when we are brokenhearted.

7. Write out Psalm 34:18 below:

8. According to Genesis 16:7, where did God find Hagar? Why do you think that is an important detail in the story?

Notice with me the description God gives Hagar in his address to her in Genesis 16:8: "slave-girl of Sarai." At this point in Hagar's story, this is her identity. God does not address her as a child of God, beloved of God, a mother, a woman. But he is not dismissing her or demeaning her. God refers to her as Sarai's slave to show Hagar he knows what she's just escaped. The God who frees slaves is speaking to someone who's just been emancipated—even if it doesn't look that way yet.

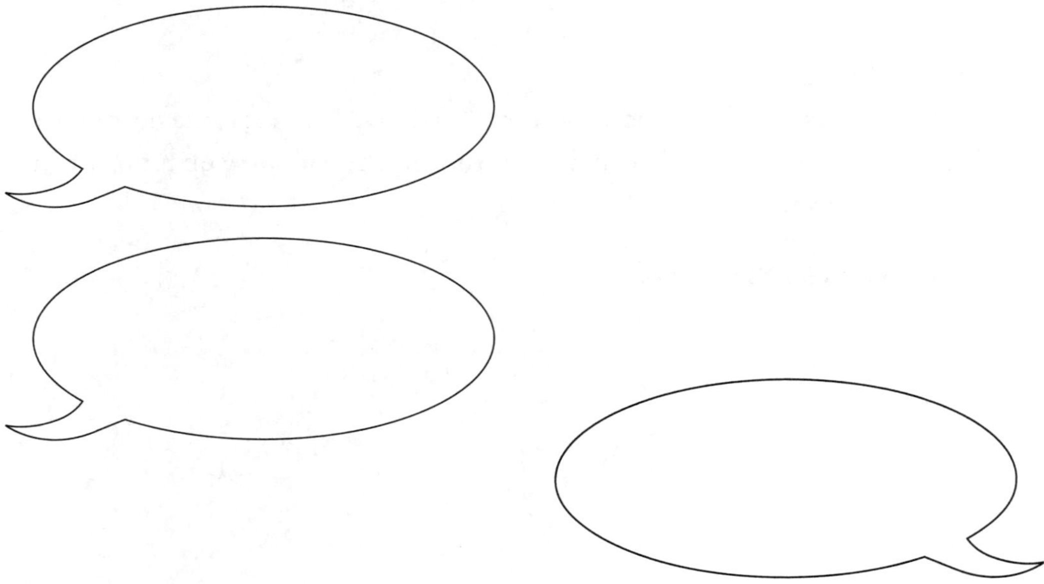

Hagar answered only one of the Lord's questions to her. She was able to communicate where she'd come from—but not where she was going. I wonder if Hagar didn't know where she was going. Or if she knew she was headed to her death and couldn't utter the words.

10. **Describe a time in your life when you had no idea where you were going but just knew you had to leave.**

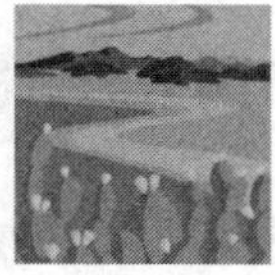

UNDERSTANDING

Now that we've finished a close reading of the Scriptures, we're going to spend some time on interpretation: doing our best to understand what God was saying to the original audience and what he's teaching us through the process. But to do so, we need to learn his ways and consider how God's Word would have been understood by the original audience before applying the same truths to our own lives. "Scripture interpretation" may sound a little stuffy, but understanding what God means to communicate to us in the Bible is crucial to enjoying a close relationship with Jesus. Part 3 will enable you to answer the question *What does it mean?*

WHAT COMES NEXT is the most distressing part of Hagar's story—when it seems as if God tells Hagar to return to abuse. At first reading, we might be tempted to interpret God's instructions to Hagar without considering God's character. But the Bible teaches that our God does not abandon those who are vulnerable.

1. Reread Genesis 16:7-16 and underline everything the Lord says to Hagar.

⁷ The angel of the LORD found her by a spring of water in the wilderness, the spring on the way to Shur. ⁸ And he said, "Hagar, slave-girl of Sarai, where have you come from and where are you going?" She said, "I am running away from my mistress Sarai." ⁹ The angel of the LORD said to her, "Return to your mistress, and submit to her." ¹⁰ The angel of the LORD also

said to her, "I will so greatly multiply your offspring that they cannot be counted for multitude." [11] And the angel of the LORD said to her,

"Now you have conceived and shall bear a son;
>   you shall call him Ishmael,
>   for the LORD has given heed to your affliction.
[12] He shall be a wild ass of a man,
with his hand against everyone,
>   and everyone's hand against him;
and he shall live at odds with all his kin."

[13] So she named the LORD who spoke to her, "You are El-roi"; for she said, "Have I really seen God and remained alive after seeing him?" [14] Therefore the well was called Beer-lahai-roi; it lies between Kadesh and Bered. [15] Hagar bore Abram a son; and Abram named his son, whom Hagar bore, Ishmael. [16] Abram was eighty-six years old when Hagar bore him Ishmael.

GENESIS 16:7-16

The difference between Hagar's return to Sarai and a person's return to an abusive situation is that Hagar was promised God's protection of her and her child. Here's a chart of God's promises to protect Hagar:

God's Promises to Protect Hagar	Practical Implications of God's Protection
"I will so greatly multiply your offspring that they cannot be counted for multitude." (Genesis 16:10)	Hagar would survive returning to Sarai because she would give birth to a child whose children would have children.
"You have conceived and shall bear a son; you shall call him Ishmael." (Genesis 16:11)	Hagar would survive returning to Sarai because she would give birth to a son and live long enough to name him.
"The LORD has given heed to your affliction." (Genesis 16:11)	God had listened to Hagar once and would listen to her again if she needed more protection.
"*He shall live* at odds with all his kin." (Genesis 16:12, emphasis added)	Hagar's child would be safe.

If you read Genesis 16 with the assumption that God wants people to sacrifice their safety or return to abusers, you'll read that into the text. But if you know God's character, you'll read extensive repetition in his promises to Hagar. God was going to protect Hagar and her son when she returned to Sarai.

If Hagar fled to escape abuse because she feared for her life or the life of her child, a return showed that she believed God, believed that his promise of protection meant the abuse would stop.

> If you are in an abusive relationship, God does not want you to suffer or submit to abuse. He wants you free and flourishing. Here's the national domestic violence hotline: 1 (800) 799-7233.

Hagar has a special place in history as the first in many categories:

+ Hagar is the first person in Scripture to flee oppression. She points to the Exodus.
+ Hagar is the first suffering servant described in Scripture. She points to Jesus.
+ Hagar is the first runaway slave. She points to Onesimus.
+ Hagar is the first woman to receive an annunciation. She points to Mary of Nazareth.
+ Hagar is the first concubine abused in Scripture (Genesis 16:6). She points to the nameless concubine in Judges 19.
+ Hagar is the first person to weep in Scripture (Genesis 21:16). She points to Jesus' tears for Lazarus.
+ Most notably, Hagar is the first and only person in the Bible to name God. Seen by God, she names him El Roi, "the God who sees."

In a world determined to dismiss the abused, wishing their cries for help would be silenced, working to diminish their experience and to render them invisible, God notices Hagar. God pays attention.

Maybe that's the message you've been aching to hear. God notices you. You are not invisible or unimportant to him. God pays attention to you. Your pain is not lost on him. The protection God offered Hagar is protection he's offered you in Christ. And if you need proof that God will do anything to protect you, to save you, look to the Cross and the empty tomb.

The Lord wants to minister to you in this moment. To be your "God who sees" in your own story.

God purposed Hagar's wilderness moments to be an encouragement to his people in future generations.

2. How would Hagar's story have impacted the original audience of Genesis, the post-Exodus Israelites?

3. How could the post-Exodus Israelites relate to the Sarai-Abram-Hagar story?

4. Write out the last four words of Genesis 16:16 below:

God was faithful to his promise to protect Hagar after her return to Sarai. Ishmael was the proof. Sadly, Hagar still had another desert in her future: the Desert of Beersheba.

Many years and several chapters later, Hagar finds herself in another desert. This time, she has not run away; she has been banished. She enters the Desert of Beersheba not because she has fled in fear—after all, she has experienced God's protection for all these years—but because she has been rejected.

5. Describe a time you've been rejected. How did that experience impact your relationships and your faith?

Between the first mention of Hagar in the Old Testament and this story, which is the last mention of her in the Old Testament, there's been enough drama to fill a season of *The Real Housewives of the Ancient Near East*. I'll do my best to summarize what happened between Genesis 16 and Genesis 21, but it is worth a read. If you have extra time, read every riveting detail and tell me the content isn't a cross between a true crime podcast and a reality TV show.

+ Circumcision is instituted as a sign of God's commitment to his people and of their identity as his beloved.
+ Ishmael is circumcised at age thirteen.
+ Sarah (no longer called Sarai) laughs at the Lord's promise to give her and Abraham (formerly Abram) a child in their old age.
+ The Lord destroys Sodom and Gomorrah for their wickedness and depravity.
+ Lot's daughters get him drunk and sleep with him to get pregnant, continuing the theme of desperate women willing to do anything to secure their futures.
+ For a second time, Abraham pawns Sarah off as his sister, this time to King Abimelech.
+ King Abimelech has more dignity and wisdom than Abraham and preserves the honor of Sarah's role as Abraham's wife.
+ Sarah has been in King Abimelech's possession long enough for him to realize that God has closed the wombs of the women in his kingdom.

The Old Testament overflow with God's forgiveness and mercy. Although the God of the old covenant is often misunderstood as harsh and punitive, the Old Testament tells a different story, one where God relentlessly loves and pursues a people whose hearts are set on sin.

Thumb through the pages of the Torah (Genesis, Exodus, Leviticus, Numbers, and Deuteronomy), and you'll discover that God is the same in the Old and New Testaments. The God of the Bible has always been and will always be slow to anger and abounding in love (Psalm 145:8-9). No matter how much drama God's people cause, the Lord works with them through their stubbornness and rebellion so that he can continue to be in relationship with them.

6. Read Genesis 21:1–21. Circle any mention of geography.

21 The LORD came to Sarah as he had said, and the LORD did for
Sarah what he had promised. ² Sarah became pregnant and bore a
son to Abraham in his old age, at the appointed time God had told him.
³ Abraham named his son who was born to him—the one Sarah bore to
him—Isaac. ⁴ When his son Isaac was eight days old, Abraham circumcised
him, as God had commanded him. ⁵ Abraham was a hundred years old
when his son Isaac was born to him.

⁶ Sarah said, "God has made me laugh, and everyone who hears will
laugh with me." ⁷ She also said, "Who would have told Abraham that
Sarah would nurse children? Yet I have borne a son for him in his old age."

⁸ The child grew and was weaned, and Abraham held a great feast
on the day Isaac was weaned. ⁹ But Sarah saw the son mocking—the one
Hagar the Egyptian had borne to Abraham. ¹⁰ So she said to Abraham,
"Drive out this slave with her son, for the son of this slave will not be a
coheir with my son Isaac!"

¹¹ This was very distressing to Abraham because of his son. ¹² But God
said to Abraham, "Do not be distressed about the boy and about your
slave. Whatever Sarah says to you, listen to her, because your offspring
will be traced through Isaac, ¹³ and I will also make a nation of the slave's
son because he is your offspring."

¹⁴ Early in the morning Abraham got up, took bread and a waterskin,
put them on Hagar's shoulders, and sent her and the boy away. She left
and wandered in the Wilderness of Beer-sheba. ¹⁵ When the water in the
skin was gone, she left the boy under one of the bushes ¹⁶ and went and
sat at a distance, about a bowshot away, for she said, "I can't bear to
watch the boy die!" While she sat at a distance, she wept loudly.

¹⁷ God heard the boy crying, and the angel of God called to Hagar from
heaven and said to her, "What's wrong, Hagar? Don't be afraid, for God
has heard the boy crying from the place where he is. ¹⁸ Get up, help the
boy up, and grasp his hand, for I will make him a great nation." ¹⁹ Then God

opened her eyes, and she saw a well. So she went and filled the waterskin and gave the boy a drink. ²⁰ God was with the boy, and he grew; he settled in the wilderness and became an archer. ²¹ He settled in the Wilderness of Paran, and his mother got a wife for him from the land of Egypt.

Sarah giving birth in her eighties or nineties—without air-conditioning, no less—is a lot to take in. Lord, have mercy. I'm at the beginning of my forties and have to travel with a foam roller for all my aches and pains.

7. What triggered Sarah's response (Genesis 21:9)? Why do you think that set her off?

8. What does Sarah ask Abraham to do with Hagar and Ishmael in Genesis 21:10?

9. What does God promise Abraham in Genesis 21:13?

10. Where did Hagar and Ishmael wander off to after being cast out of their family?

11. What more could Abraham have done to protect Hagar and Ishmael?

Because Ishmael was circumcised at thirteen, we know he was older than that at this point in his life. Hagar was not casting aside a baby but laying down a young man who was dying from thirst. Hagar laying her son down for his final rest was an agonizing moment for them both.

12. Based on Genesis 21:16–17, who was crying?

☐ Hagar

☐ Ishmael

☐ both

I wonder what this moment in the desert sounded like. Imagining the pain they were enduring is heart-wrenching.

Hagar couldn't bear the sight of her son's death any more than you or I would be able to. She was about to lose her most precious love, her future, and her faith in the God who had seen her in a different desert but seemed to abandon her to this one.

13. What threatened Hagar's and Ishmael's lives in the Desert of Beersheba?

14. How does Hagar and Ishmael's Desert of Beersheba story resonate with you? (If you've ever lost a child, I am so sorry. It was never supposed to be this way.)

15. What does God do for Hagar in Genesis 21:19?

I find it comforting that the angel of God asked Hagar what was wrong. God already knew, of course. But one of the kindest gifts God gives his people is listening to their stories from their point of view.

16. What do Hagar's desert stories teach us about God's commitment to keeping his promises?

HAGAR'S DESERT EXPERIENCES

Hagar in the Desert of Shur	Hagar in the Desert of Beersheba
pregnant with Ishmael	accompanied by teenage Ishmael
escaping Sarai's abuse	exiled by Sarah out of disdain
God asking Hagar, "Where have you come from and where are you going?" (Genesis 16:8)	God asking Hagar, "What troubles you?" (Genesis 21:17)
God providing a spring with water for her to drink from	God providing a well with water for her to drink from

✦ ✦ ✦

In every lesson, we'll expand our storyline chart to trace the desert locations we are studying together.

THE DESERTS STORYLINE OF SCRIPTURE

Location	Words from God for Desert Seasons	On the Other Side of the Desert
The Deserts of Shur and Beersheba (Genesis 16, 21)	[The angel of the LORD said,] "Where have you come from and where are you going?" (Genesis 16:8) [The angel of God said,] "What troubles you?" (Genesis 21:17)	Hagar went through rejection to get to protection.
The Desert of Dothan (Genesis 37, 45, 50)	[Joseph said,] "Do not be afraid! Am I in the place of God? Even though you intended to do harm to me, God intended it for good." (Genesis 50:19–20)	Joseph's brothers went through resentment to get to forgiveness.
The Desert of Sinai (Numbers 11, 14)	[The LORD said,] "How long will this people despise me? And how long will they refuse to believe in me, in spite of all the signs that I have done among them?" (Numbers 14:11)	The Israelites went through insecurity to get to belonging.
The Desert of Judea (Matthew 3–4)	[Jesus said,] "It is written, 'Do not put the Lord your God to the test.'" (Matthew 4:7)	Jesus went through trials to get to ministry.
The Deserts of Ministry (Matthew 14, 15)	[Jesus asked,] "How many loaves have you?" (Matthew 15:34)	The disciples went through scarcity to get to abundance.

1. What about Hagar's two desert stories resonates with you most? What part of her story piques your curiosity?

2. What did you learn about God in this lesson? And what did you learn about yourself in this lesson?

3. How should these truths shape your faith community and change you?

RESPONDING

The purpose of Bible study is to help you become more Christlike; that's why part 4 will include journaling space for your reflection on and responses to the content and a blank checklist for actionable next steps. You'll be able to process what you're learning so that you can live out the concepts and pursue Christlikeness. Part 4 will enable you to answer the questions *What truths is this passage teaching?* and *How do I apply this to my life?*

I'VE JUST FINISHED a record-breaking week of rejection. By any measure, it was a pile-on. My circumstances are too tender to describe right now, but I will share that more than once in the last five days I sobbed hot, ugly tears until I was delirious with pity laughter. By the time you read this, I'll be years past the disappointment. But right now, as I gather myself, I'm intentionally choosing to process my pain with Christ. Which is to say that I'm needing to recenter my attention on Jesus throughout my day, every day, so that I make it through this desert moment.

As I reflected upon the Desert of Shur, the Desert of Beersheba, and Hagar's harrowing journeys through both, I zeroed in on God's questions to Hagar in her wilderness wanderings. What does God choose to say to someone who has suffered the worst rejection imaginable? How did he address Hagar's pain? God asked questions. Three of them, to be exact. And I've spent time meditating on God's questions to Hagar, imagining they're directed at me.

Usually in this section, you and I get to this point in the lesson and look at three key takeaways, and we'll be doing that in the other four weeks of the study. But I sensed we needed to do something different in this first lesson. I'm going to show you my answers to these questions from God, straight from my journal, and I'm going to leave space for you to journal your own answers to these questions. There's no right or wrong way to express yourself on the page. You can draw, list bullet points, or write long form.

The exercise was just what I needed, and I hope it serves you.

1. WHERE HAVE YOU COME FROM?

Lord, before I landed in the desert of rejection, I was already on a downhill slope of exhaustion. Showing up for the people I love in this season is especially taxing because I'm running on empty. But the harder part to admit to you is that I'm coming from a place of insecurity. All the rejection has me feeling misunderstood, and I'm rehearsing imaginary conversations justifying myself. Shame, pride, and self-protection are heavy burdens to bear on my own. Maybe that's the point. I'm coming from a place of self-protection, and I need to trust that you're going to shoulder my burdens with me so that the load gets lighter.

2. WHERE ARE YOU GOING?

Lord, I'm still on a mission to spark holy curiosity in Bible readers, but one pathway to do so has been closed. I really thought the path you had me on would be longer. I only want to go to the places where I'm following you.

3. WHAT'S WRONG?

Lord, this dream ended so much sooner than I anticipated. I'm troubled by self-doubt, loss of sleep, and sadness. And I'm troubled that I wasn't taken seriously. That brings up so many old wounds.

Use this journaling space to process what you are learning.

Ask yourself how these truths impact your relationship with God and with others.

What is the Holy Spirit bringing to your mind as actionable next steps in your faith journey?

✦

✦

✦

GOING THROUGH RESENTMENT TO GET TO FORGIVENESS

**THE DESERT OF DOTHAN:
WHERE JOSEPH GETS THROWN INTO A PIT**

SCRIPTURE: GENESIS 37, 45, 50

CONTEXT

Before you begin your study, we will start with the context of the story we are about to read together: the setting, both cultural and historical; the people involved; and where our passage fits in the larger setting of Scripture. All these things help us make sense of what we're reading. Understanding the context of a Bible story is fundamental to reading Scripture well. Getting your bearings before you read will enable you to answer the question *What am I about to read?*

I'VE MENTIONED what a big fan my son is of the Marvel movies, which is how I know this: Tony Stark (otherwise known as Iron Man) and Steve Rogers (otherwise known as Captain America) were friends until they weren't. The rift between them is resolved, though, when Tony admits to Steve, "Turns out resentment is corrosive, and I hate it."[1]

Resentment eats away at our souls and undermines our well-being. Like unforgiveness, resentment doesn't just happen—no one becomes resentful unless they've been treated unfairly. But when we keep a record of wrongs, the person behaving unjustly doesn't suffer. We do.

Resentment occupies brain space we need to be free to worship God and love others, clouding our judgment with suspicion and making our insides sour with bitterness. Once we've been treated unjustly, unresolved resentment starts a chain reaction like a trail of dominoes tumbling over. Negative feelings toward the person who wronged us topple over onto anyone else we're afraid might hurt us. Eventually those fears pile up into barriers that keep us from authentic, meaningful, and reciprocal relationships. What began as a wound from a loved one or a leader or someone we trust sends us and the people we love into a desert of resentment.

In this lesson we are going to meditate on a pivotal moment in the life of Joseph. While most of the details we have about Joseph's life come from his time living in Egypt, we're going to zero in on a stunning betrayal in the wilderness: when his brothers threw him into a pit in the Desert of Dothan. Joseph's experience in the Desert of Dothan lasted a few minutes, maybe a few hours. And this desert is not what you might picture—expansive, seemingly unending mounds of sand like in the Sahara. The Desert of Dothan was small and was near lush vegetation that attracted livestock owners to come nourish their animals.

Joseph's brothers were consumed with resentment toward him, and as a result, they schemed to murder him. The scene is short, but the consequences of the story had a lasting impact on everyone involved. It might sound a bit extreme, but this is where unchecked resentment leads: death. Death of relationships, trust, vulnerability, and freedom.

Like the desert in Hagar's story, Joseph's desert represents the hard places in life we have to go through to get to better days. In between Hagar's experience with rejection in the Deserts of Shur and Beersheba and Joseph's experience with resentment in the Desert of Dothan are many chapters (Genesis 22–36) summarizing two generations in Abraham's family: Abraham to Isaac and Isaac to Jacob. The theme of this section of Genesis is *schemes*.

Genesis 22–36

+ Isaac schemes to pass off Rebekah as his sister instead of his wife. (Sound familiar?)
+ Rebekah and her son Jacob scheme to deceive Isaac for Esau's birthright.
+ Laban schemes to deceive Jacob by replacing Rachel with Leah on Jacob's wedding night.
+ Dinah's brothers, Jacob's sons, scheme to deceive the people of the city of Shechem with circumcision after Dinah is raped by a man named Shechem.

The first faith family was messed up. There's no denying it. But through it all, God was faithful to this family who'd been commissioned to bless all people with God's love, which shows us that their dysfunction is not the main point of the book of Genesis. The point is that God can restore brokenness. Whether the brokenness is inside us, being done to us, or shared through family dynamics, God can heal and restore.

You're about to read the little we know about Joseph's relationship with his brothers before he became a slave in Egypt. And what I hope you see is the relentless commitment God has to people wandering through life.

God wants to get you through resentment to get you to forgiveness.

1. **PERSONAL CONTEXT: What is going on in your life right now that might impact how you understand Joseph's story in the Desert of Dothan? What do you hope to learn from this lesson?**

2. **SPIRITUAL CONTEXT: If you've never studied Joseph's story in the Desert of Dothan before, what piques your curiosity? If you've studied this place or Joseph before, what impressions and insights do you recall?**

3. **BIBLICAL CONTEXT: What questions come to mind as you read about the context of Joseph's story? What questions do you wish you could have answered before studying this part of Scripture?**

SEEING

Seeing the text is vital if we want the heart of the Scripture passage to sink in. We read slowly and intentionally through the text with the context in mind. As we practice close, thoughtful reading of Scripture, we pick up on phrases, implications, and meanings we might otherwise have missed. Part 2 includes close Scripture reading and observation questions to empower you to answer the question *What is the story saying?*

1. **Read Genesis 37. Underline any geographical markers in the story.**

37 Jacob settled in the land where his father had lived as an alien, the land of Canaan. ² This is the story of the family of Jacob.

Joseph, being seventeen years old, was shepherding the flock with his brothers; he was a helper to the sons of Bilhah and Zilpah, his father's wives; and Joseph brought a bad report of them to their father. ³ Now Israel loved Joseph more than any other of his children, because he was the son of his old age; and he had made him a long robe with sleeves. ⁴ But when his brothers saw that their father loved him more than all his brothers, they hated him, and could not speak peaceably to him.

⁵ Once Joseph had a dream, and when he told it to his brothers, they hated him even more. ⁶ He said to them, "Listen to this dream that I

dreamed. ⁷ There we were, binding sheaves in the field. Suddenly my sheaf rose and stood upright; then your sheaves gathered around it, and bowed down to my sheaf." ⁸ His brothers said to him, "Are you indeed to reign over us? Are you indeed to have dominion over us?" So they hated him even more because of his dreams and his words.

⁹ He had another dream, and told it to his brothers, saying, "Look, I have had another dream: the sun, the moon, and eleven stars were bowing down to me." ¹⁰ But when he told it to his father and to his brothers, his father rebuked him, and said to him, "What kind of dream is this that you have had? Shall we indeed come, I and your mother and your brothers, and bow to the ground before you?" ¹¹ So his brothers were jealous of him, but his father kept the matter in mind.

¹² Now his brothers went to pasture their father's flock near Shechem. ¹³ And Israel said to Joseph, "Are not your brothers pasturing the flock at Shechem? Come, I will send you to them." He answered, "Here I am." ¹⁴ So he said to him, "Go now, see if it is well with your brothers and with the flock; and bring word back to me." So he sent him from the valley of Hebron.

He came to Shechem, ¹⁵ and a man found him wandering in the fields; the man asked him, "What are you seeking?" ¹⁶ "I am seeking my brothers," he said; "tell me, please, where they are pasturing the flock." ¹⁷ The man said, "They have gone away, for I heard them say, 'Let us go to Dothan.'" So Joseph went after his brothers, and found them at Dothan. ¹⁸ They saw him from a distance, and before he came near to them, they conspired to kill him. ¹⁹ They said to one another, "Here comes this dreamer. ²⁰ Come now, let us kill him and throw him into one of the pits; then we shall say that a wild animal has devoured him, and we shall see what will become of his dreams." ²¹ But when Reuben heard it, he delivered him out of their hands, saying, "Let us not take his life." ²² Reuben said to them, "Shed no blood; throw him into this pit here in the wilderness, but lay no hand on him"—that he might rescue him out of their hand and restore him to his father. 23 So when Joseph came to his brothers, they stripped him of his robe, the long robe with sleeves that he wore; 24 and they took him and threw him into a pit. The pit was empty; there was no water in it.

25 Then they sat down to eat; and looking up they saw a caravan of Ishmaelites coming from Gilead, with their camels carrying gum, balm, and resin, on their way to carry it down to Egypt. 26 Then Judah said to his brothers, "What profit is it if we kill our brother and conceal his blood? 27 Come, let us sell him to the Ishmaelites, and not lay our hands on him, for he is our brother, our own flesh." And his brothers agreed. 28 When some Midianite traders passed by, they drew Joseph up, lifting him out of the pit, and sold him to the Ishmaelites for twenty pieces of silver. And they took Joseph to Egypt.

29 When Reuben returned to the pit and saw that Joseph was not in the pit, he tore his clothes. 30 He returned to his brothers, and said, "The boy is gone; and I, where can I turn?" 31 Then they took Joseph's robe, slaughtered a goat, and dipped the robe in the blood. 32 They had the long robe with sleeves taken to their father, and they said, "This we have found; see now whether it is your son's robe or not." 33 He recognized it, and said, "It is my son's robe! A wild animal has devoured him; Joseph is without doubt torn to pieces." 34 Then Jacob tore his garments, and put sackcloth on his loins, and mourned for his son many days. 35 All his sons and all his daughters sought to comfort him; but he refused to be comforted, and said, "No, I shall go down to Sheol to my son, mourning." Thus his father bewailed him. 36 Meanwhile the Midianites had sold him in Egypt to Potiphar, one of Pharaoh's officials, the captain of the guard.

GENESIS 37

If I were to sum up this story, I'd say it is about Joseph's brothers' resentment leading to his enslavement. But the author of Genesis, under the inspiration of the Holy Spirit, tells us the bigger story.

2. Fill in the blank below from Genesis 37:2:

This is the story of _______________________ .

Since the chapter numbers are not original to the text of the Bible, Genesis 37:2 could be part of the previous chapter's topic and a less natural starting point for the new chapter. Nonetheless, this sentence is the link between what has happened in the past and what is about to happen to Joseph.

The only other child of Jacob to get their own chapter in Genesis thus far is Dinah, who was raped by a man named Shechem in a place called Shechem (Genesis 34). At the end of Dinah's story, Joseph's brothers commit mass murder of the people of Shechem as retribution.

The author of Genesis assumes that you and I, and the ancient readers of Joseph's story, are thinking about the rest of Jacob's children and how the rape of Dinah impacted the whole family. How the vengeful violence of Jacob's sons upon the city of Shechem led to mass murder. How Jacob's sons are capable of murder.

Why is Joseph's story really a story about the family of Jacob? It's not only because Joseph was one of Jacob's sons but also because up until this point Jacob's kids have been either victimized or creating victims. And the last time their family got close to the city of Shechem, they were all in danger (Genesis 38). A story about the family of Jacob is a horror story, and the author wants to set an ominous stage for what comes next.

3. List anything you learn about Joseph from Genesis 37:1-3.

✦

✦

✦

Two details that stand out to me are that Joseph was a snitch and that Joseph was his father's favorite. And Joseph's brothers hated him for it. They were so consumed with hate that they couldn't speak to Joseph without disrupting the peace in the family. The themes at play in the story are sibling rivalry and parental favoritism.

Of course, Joseph did himself no favors. Take off the coat, bro, and read the room. Whether Joseph was prideful, immature, or obtuse, we can't be sure—but something compelled him to tell his family about not one but *two* dreams implying that he would one day rule over his family in a position of authority. Who could stomach that kind of smugness? You can imagine Reuben face-palming as Joseph explains his dreams to the rest of the brothers or motioning to Joseph to cut off the speech to save his dignity.

4. **Write out the last sentence of Genesis 37:8 and answer this question: How did Joseph's brothers process his first prophetic dream?**

5. **Based on Genesis 37:11, how did Joseph's brothers process his second prophetic dream?**

6. **List any emotional responses Joseph's brothers had to Joseph. How might these reactions have led to their conspiracy to murder him?**

✦

✦

✦

I've wondered if the plot to kill Joseph was less about killing Joseph and more about killing the possibility that his dreams would come true. The irony of ironies is that their resentful scheming—switched from murder to enslavement—became God's pathway to fulfilling the prophetic visions.

7. **Write out what Joseph's brothers say to each other in Genesis 37:19 as Joseph approaches them in the Desert of Dothan:**

The eldest brother, Reuben, tried to save Joseph's life by suggesting that instead of killing Joseph, the brothers should throw him into a pit and leave him in the desert to die. Reuben had every intention of coming back to pull Joseph out once everyone's temper had cooled down. But once Reuben was gone, the angry mob of remaining brothers opted to sell Joseph into slavery, making him the first Hebrew victim of human trafficking mentioned in the Bible. Sadly, slavery was a common Ancient Near Eastern practice, but this is the first mention of a Hebrew (a future Israelite) subjected to the dehumanization of being sold as property. The original readers of the book of Genesis, the post-Exodus Israelites wandering in the wilderness, had themselves known the trauma of Joseph's experience in the slave trade. His journey toward Egypt as a slave was the prelude to their journey out of Egypt in freedom.

8. According to Genesis 37:33, what did Jacob assume had happened to Joseph based on the blood-soaked coat?

No wild animal had mauled Joseph, but Joseph's brothers had been wild and beastly in their actions and lie. In this narrative, Joseph's clothing serves as more than just a useful tool for their deceit. According to Dr. Leland Ryken, "The clothing of Joseph indicates transition points in the story and foreshadows the next phase of the hero's career."[2]

JOSEPH'S GARMENT PATTERN

Scene	Significance
Jacob gives Joseph a sleeved robe (Genesis 37:3).	This special robe symbolizes Jacob's favoritism and foreshadows the sibling rivalry that unfolds.
Joseph is disrobed by his brothers (Genesis 37:23).	This disrobing scene signals Joseph's break from his family and home.
Potiphar's wife grabs Joseph's clothes (Genesis 39:12).	This disrobing by Potiphar's scheming wife signals Joseph's fall from favor.
Joseph changes his clothes to appear before Pharaoh (Genesis 41:14).	This clothing change signals that Joseph's favor is about to change.
Joseph is clothed in garments of fine linen (Genesis 41:42).	These fine linen garments demonstrate Joseph's elevation to a position of power and authority.
Joseph gives festal garments at the reunion scene with his brothers (Genesis 45:22).	These celebratory garments signal the restoration of the family.

In the desert, Joseph was stripped of his symbol of his father's favor—and yet it was in the desert that God set Joseph on the path toward becoming who God had made him to be. The Desert of Dothan was not the end for Joseph. But the deserts of Egypt still lay before him.

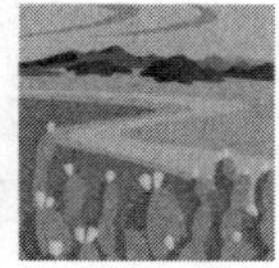

UNDERSTANDING

Now that we've finished a close reading of the Scriptures, we're going to spend some time on interpretation: doing our best to understand what God was saying to the original audience and what he's teaching us through the process. But to do so, we need to learn his ways and consider how God's Word would have been understood by the original audience before applying the same truths to our own lives. "Scripture interpretation" may sound a little stuffy, but understanding what God means to communicate to us in the Bible is crucial to enjoying a close relationship with Jesus. Part 3 will enable you to answer the question *What does it mean?*

MY HEART GOES OUT to those of you who know what it's like to grow up with family dysfunction and those of you who know the pain of hate among siblings that leads to verbal abuse and, in some cases, physical violence.

1. **When was the last time you struggled to speak peaceably with a sibling or other family member? Describe why it was such a challenge.**

2. Have you ever been given the silent treatment or experienced verbal abuse? How
    did that impact you, your faith, and your relationships?

Joseph's family dysfunction brought him to a pit in the Desert of Dothan. His brothers sold him into slavery like a commodity, as if he were as valuable to them as gum, balm, or resin.

3. Has anyone ever made you feel unworthy or without any value? Describe that
    experience and how it impacted you.

4. How do you imagine that this experience impacted Joseph?

5. What about his brothers—how do you imagine selling Joseph into slavery impacted them?

If you were one of Joseph's brothers, would you ever be able to trust those around you again? Did Reuben wonder if his brothers could turn on him the way they'd turned on Joseph?

Even though it was Joseph who was thrown into the pit in the wilderness and then exiled to Egypt, the next thirteen chapters of Genesis detail the ways Joseph's brothers tried to climb out of the metaphorical pits they'd all dug for themselves by betraying their brother and lying to their father. And to think it all started with hatred, jealousy, and resentment.

The next time Joseph saw his brothers, the whole land felt like a desert. Joseph was now in a position of power and authority after correctly interpreting dreams for Pharaoh and predicting a famine that would impact, along with the rest of the known world, his own family. Joseph became highly regarded by the Egyptians as wise, discerning, and filled with the Spirit of God. Because of God working through Joseph, Egypt had prepared for the famine and become a destination for starving people from surrounding lands. Among these people were Jacob's sons, who had journeyed to Egypt to buy grain.

Unchecked resentment had led Joseph's brothers to set a death trap for their brother in the desert. Joseph, now with more power than his brothers could dream of, could have let resentment fester and rule him as well. But instead, he chose forgiveness and offered them a lifeline. In a riveting scene, Joseph reveals his identity to his brothers, who haven't seen him in over two decades.

6. Read Genesis 45:1-15. Underline any mention of crying.

45 Then Joseph could no longer control himself before all those who stood by him, and he cried out, "Send everyone away from me." So no one stayed with him when Joseph made himself known to his brothers. [2] And he wept so loudly that the Egyptians heard it, and the household of Pharaoh heard it. [3] Joseph said to his brothers, "I am Joseph. Is my father still alive?" But his brothers could not answer him, so dismayed were they at his presence.

[4] Then Joseph said to his brothers, "Come closer to me." And they came closer. He said, "I am your brother, Joseph, whom you sold into Egypt. [5] And now do not be distressed, or angry with yourselves, because you sold me here; for God sent me before you to preserve life. [6] For the famine has been in the land these two years; and there are five more years in which there will be neither plowing nor harvest. [7] God sent me before you to preserve for you a remnant on earth, and to keep alive for you many survivors. [8] So it was not you who sent me here, but God; he has made me a father to Pharaoh, and lord of all his house and ruler over all the land of Egypt. [9] Hurry and go up to my father and say to him, 'Thus says your son Joseph, God has made me lord of all Egypt; come down to me, do not delay. [10] You shall settle in the land of Goshen, and you shall be near me, you and your children and your children's children, as well as your flocks, your herds, and all that you have. [11] I will provide for you there—since there are five more years of famine to come—so that you and your household, and all that you have, will not come to poverty.' [12] And now your eyes and the eyes of my brother Benjamin see that it is my own mouth that speaks to you. [13] You must tell my father how greatly I am honored in Egypt, and all that you have seen. Hurry and bring my father down here." [14] Then he fell upon his brother Benjamin's neck and wept, while Benjamin wept upon his neck. [15] And he kissed all his brothers and wept upon them; and after that his brothers talked with him.

GENESIS 45:1-15

7. **How would you describe what happens between Joseph and his brothers in Genesis 45:14–15?**

8. **Compare Genesis 45:14–15 with Genesis 37:23–24. What difference do you see?**

The takeaway from Joseph's story is certainly not that you should seek restoration with someone in your family who has tried to kill you. Forgiveness does not always lead to restoration. Sometimes it leads to stronger boundaries. Sometimes a severed relationship is the healthiest path forward. But I do want you to notice a few things that had changed in Joseph's story to make restoration between him and his brothers possible:

+ The power dynamic had shifted. Joseph was no longer weaker than his older brothers. He was one of the most powerful men in authority in the only world power with food enough to feed the masses. Joseph was no longer vulnerable.

+ Joseph had worked through his brothers' resentment and his own temptation toward resentment in return. The last time Joseph had been with his brothers, they were throwing him into a pit out of resentment, but now Joseph is choosing to fall upon his brothers to weep and kiss them in restoration.

+ It took many tests of character for Joseph to trust his brothers again. He waited to see demonstration of the fact that they had changed; their protection of Benjamin—who, as the only other son of Joseph's mother, Rachel, was most likely to be Jacob's favorite and thus another potential victim of the brothers' jealousy—showed Joseph that they had.

So far in the biblical story, deserts, or wildernesses, are the pit stops of life. The wastelands no one wants to wander through alone. In other stories throughout the Old Testament, deserts are the site of danger, death, rebellion, punishment, and temptation.[4] Simply put, you don't want to find yourself in a desert in a Bible story. But in case you do find yourself in a desert, Joseph proves to us that God comes to our rescue. God provides a way through the wilderness. And when the time comes, God equips us to move through death-dealing resentment and into the restoration of forgiveness.

There is one more important theological message in Joseph's story I want to highlight. What happened to Joseph foreshadowed what happened to the nation of Israel: They were enslaved by the Egyptians. You and I are reading this story knowing what is coming next—freedom from slavery in the book of Exodus— but the original audience would have been looking back on history to understand more about God through the telling of Joseph's story.

Joseph's story means that you and I can be confident in God's freeing power.

9. **Write out Genesis 45:5 below:**

10. After all these years, how did Joseph view his hardships?

God can work miracles through suffering. Which is not to say that we should invite suffering into our lives or bypass our feelings but rather that we can name the harm done to us and also accept God's providence as a means to redemption in suffering.

This moment in Genesis 45 shows us that Joseph's brothers, on the other hand, needed reassurance that Joseph was forgiving. That's why the very last chapter of Genesis is another reunion scene where the brothers fear that Joseph has not fully forgiven the past.

11. Read Genesis 50:15–21 and underline anything Joseph says to his brothers.

¹⁵ Realizing that their father was dead, Joseph's brothers said, "What if Joseph still bears a grudge against us and pays us back in full for all the wrong that we did to him?" ¹⁶ So they approached Joseph, saying, "Your father gave this instruction before he died, ¹⁷ 'Say to Joseph: I beg you, forgive the crime of your brothers and the wrong they did in harming you.'

Now therefore please forgive the crime of the servants of the God of your father." Joseph wept when they spoke to him. [18] Then his brothers also wept, fell down before him, and said, "We are here as your slaves." [19] But Joseph said to them, "Do not be afraid! Am I in the place of God? [20] Even though you intended to do harm to me, God intended it for good, in order to preserve a numerous people, as he is doing today. [21] So have no fear; I myself will provide for you and your little ones." In this way he reassured them, speaking kindly to them.

GENESIS 50:15-21

12. Describe a time in your life when you experienced relational restoration.

The story of Joseph (Gen. 37, 39–46, 50) is built around an important character type of biblical literature, the suffering servant. Such a hero undergoes suffering, usually undeserved, that accomplishes great good for other people. Joseph is such an innocent sufferer who becomes a savior of people. His story is dominated by the theme of providence. Although events that happen to the hero seem at the time to be tragic, by the time the story is over they turn out to have been governed by God for a redemptive purpose.[5]

Leland Ryken, *Words of Delight*

The last layer of Joseph's wilderness story I want to explore together is Joseph's character type: suffering servant. Joseph foreshadows Christ, the ultimate suffering servant.

+ Joseph was unjustly betrayed by his brothers and became an innocent victim of the slave trade, and Jesus was unjustly betrayed by Judas and became an innocent victim of the Roman Empire.

+ Joseph was falsely accused of sexual misconduct by Potiphar's wife and jailed for years for a crime he didn't commit, and Jesus suffered crucifixion despite Pilate's acknowledgment that Jesus had committed no sin.

+ Joseph was humiliated and then elevated into a position of influence, and Jesus endured the humiliation of the Cross and then rose from the dead in triumphal victory over evil powers.

+ Joseph forgave his brothers, and Jesus forgives us.

13. Read Isaiah 53 and underline any reference to the suffering servant being betrayed, accused, and humiliated.

53 Who has believed what we have heard?
   And to whom has the arm of the LORD been revealed?
² For he grew up before him like a young plant,
   and like a root out of dry ground;
he had no form or majesty that we should look at him,
   nothing in his appearance that we should desire him.

[3] He was despised and rejected by others;
    a man of suffering and acquainted with infirmity;
and as one from whom others hide their faces
    he was despised, and we held him of no account.

[4] Surely he has borne our infirmities
    and carried our diseases;
yet we accounted him stricken,
    struck down by God, and afflicted.
[5] But he was wounded for our transgressions,
    crushed for our iniquities;
upon him was the punishment that made us whole,
    and by his bruises we are healed.
[6] All we like sheep have gone astray;
    we have all turned to our own way,
and the Lord has laid on him
    the iniquity of us all.

[7] He was oppressed, and he was afflicted,
    yet he did not open his mouth;
like a lamb that is led to the slaughter,
    and like a sheep that before its shearers is silent,
    so he did not open his mouth.
[8] By a perversion of justice he was taken away.
    Who could have imagined his future?
For he was cut off from the land of the living,
    stricken for the transgression of my people.
[9] They made his grave with the wicked
    and his tomb with the rich,
although he had done no violence,
    and there was no deceit in his mouth.

¹⁰ Yet it was the will of the LORD to crush him with pain.

When you make his life an offering for sin,

    he shall see his offspring, and shall prolong his days;

through him the will of the LORD shall prosper.

    ¹¹ Out of his anguish he shall see light;

he shall find satisfaction through his knowledge.

    The righteous one, my servant, shall make many righteous,

    and he shall bear their iniquities.

¹² Therefore I will allot him a portion with the great,

    and he shall divide the spoil with the strong;

because he poured out himself to death,

    and was numbered with the transgressors;

yet he bore the sin of many,

    and made intercession for the transgressors.

ISAIAH 53

14. Journal below a response to Isaiah 53 after you spend a few minutes reflecting on Christ's fulfillment of these prophetic words.

✦ ✦ ✦

Let's check back in on our Deserts Storyline.

THE DESERTS STORYLINE OF SCRIPTURE

Location	Words from God for Desert Seasons	On the Other Side of the Desert
The Deserts of Shur and Beersheba (Genesis 16, 21)	[The angel of the LORD said,] "Where have you come from and where are you going?" (Genesis 16:8) [The angel of God said,] "What troubles you?" (Genesis 21:17)	Hagar went through rejection to get to protection.
The Desert of Dothan (Genesis 37, 45, 50)	[Joseph said,] "Do not be afraid! Am I in the place of God? Even though you intended to do harm to me, God intended it for good." (Genesis 50:19-20)	Joseph's brothers went through resentment to get to forgiveness.
The Desert of Sinai (Numbers 11, 14)	[The LORD said,] "How long will this people despise me? And how long will they refuse to believe in me, in spite of all the signs that I have done among them?" (Numbers 14:11)	The Israelites went through insecurity to get to belonging.
The Desert of Judea (Matthew 3–4)	[Jesus said,] "It is written, 'Do not put the Lord your God to the test.'" (Matthew 4:7)	Jesus went through trials to get to ministry.
The Deserts of Ministry (Matthew 14, 15)	[Jesus asked,] "How many loaves have you?" (Matthew 15:34)	The disciples went through scarcity to get to abundance.

1. What about Joseph's Desert of Dothan story resonates with you most? What part of the story piques your curiosity?

2. What did you learn about God in this lesson? And what did you learn about yourself in this lesson?

3. How should these truths shape your faith community and change you?

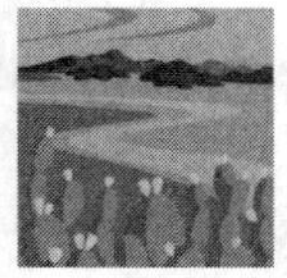

RESPONDING

The purpose of Bible study is to help you become more Christlike; that's why part 4 will include journaling space for your reflection on and responses to the content and a blank checklist for actionable next steps. You'll be able to process what you're learning so that you can live out the concepts and pursue Christlikeness. Part 4 will enable you to answer the questions *What truths is this passage teaching?* and *How do I apply this to my life?*

WE WOULD PROBABLY have understood if Joseph had chosen to harbor resentment or keep receipts of all his brothers' wrongdoings. But instead Joseph treated his brothers the way they should have treated him. He forgave the people who'd harmed him. He broke the cycle! With newfound agency and authority, Joseph was able to pursue reconciliation with his brothers—because Joseph realized that God's redemptive power can transform even the most wounding experiences into opportunities for grace.

I wish I could tell you that I'm skilled at emulating Joseph's brothers' journey through resentment to forgiveness and restoration. But I'm learning—slowly, surely—that I can't stay in the wilderness of resentment. I'll die there. I need out of the desert, and so do you.

Is there someone you argue with or zing with one-liners in your head? Do you still rehearse a past hurtful conversation but with an alternate ending where you get the last word? Are you distracted with thoughts of the people who have hurt you? If so, my heart is tender toward you. Your backstory might resemble Joseph's. But so can the path ahead. Here's what I would offer to you.

1. YOUR DESERT DROP DOESN'T DEFINE YOU.

What you've been through does not define you. You are not the wounded one, the left-for-dead, the broken one. You are not fated to failure or destined for destruction. You are the beloved. You are the one God rescued from the pit of despair. You're the one he left the ninety-nine for. You are his pride and glory, and no one can take your identity from you. And remember, what God has already done in your life has made you more resilient, capable, and wise.

2. GOD INTENDS GOOD FOR YOU.

God intends for you to experience good in this life. In fact, God's Word says that goodness and mercy are trailing you like a shadow (Psalm 23:6). This is not to say that the hard things you've lived through were good. Or that it will be smooth sailing from here on out. What God's Word teaches is that despite the darkness present in our world, our good God is the Light of the World, the lamp unto our feet as we keep moving forward.

Joseph's story shows us a pathway to forgiveness and restoration. A road map of grace. The goal is not to become more like Joseph but to recognize God's goodness, his staying presence with Joseph before, during, and after the time Joseph was shoved into a pit in the Desert of Dothan. Joseph's time in the pit had nothing good in it, but through the long wilderness of slavery and imprisonment, God was with him. And God turned his tears into joy.

Your life will keep getting interrupted and redirected by God's outstretched hand so that you enjoy his goodness. If you are angry at God because of your circumstances, know this truth: Resenting God means we keep his goodness at arm's length. Now is the time to restore your relationship with Christ by accepting that his intentions for you are pure. You can trust God.

3. RESENTMENT IS CORROSIVE; RESTORATION IS HEALING.

Resentment is a silent killer. You might be so practiced at covering it up or faking peace that no one knows just how much you're suffering. Resentment shows up in your life as a plastered, inauthentic smile when you'd rather stick out your tongue or roll your eyes. Resentment is reviewing an imaginary list of grievances and ticking off the bulleted items with new proof that the other person is still wrong and you are still right.

Yes, whoever hurt you was wrong. That's the plain and simple truth. They don't get a pass for their behavior. But you can trust God's oversight on the matter. God will deal with them. Leave vengeance to the Lord's judgment. Don't mess with resentment—it is a desert place that won't sustain a fruitful life.

If you choose to forgive and let go of the pain, freedom will be an ongoing, lifelong practice that won't happen overnight. But when you opt to go *through* resentment *to get to* forgiveness, you'll find restoration to God, to others, and to yourself waiting on the other side. Ask God to heal your wounds—spiritual, emotional, physical, mental. Invite his healing power into your life, and kick resentment to the curb.

Use this journaling space to process what you are learning.

Ask yourself how these truths impact your relationship with God and with others.

What is the Holy Spirit bringing to your mind as actionable next steps in your faith journey?

✦

✦

✦

GOING THROUGH INSECURITY TO GET TO BELONGING

THE DESERT OF SINAI:
WHERE MOSES AND THE ISRAELITES WANDER IN THE WILDERNESS

SCRIPTURE: NUMBERS 11, 14

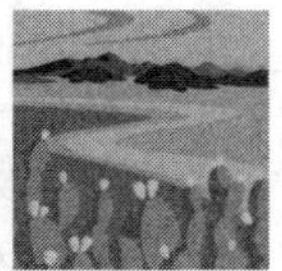

CONTEXT

Before you begin your study, we will start with the context of the story we are about to read together: the setting, both cultural and historical; the people involved; and where our passage fits in the larger setting of Scripture. All these things help us make sense of what we're reading. Understanding the context of a Bible story is fundamental to reading Scripture well. Getting your bearings before you read will enable you to answer the question *What am I about to read?*

WE CAN'T STUDY DESERTS in the Bible without camping out in the book of Numbers. You might be feeling some trepidation, but imagine me motioning for you to squint into the future. To see past the endless census lists that usually cause us to skip the book and move on to Deuteronomy.

Because, you see, in Hebrew, Numbers is titled "In the Wilderness." If we set our gaze on the middle of the book of Numbers, we see God's people wandering in the desert. Or, should I say, rebelling in the desert.

A lot has happened between our last desert story of Joseph in Dothan and the desert stories we are going to read in the book of Numbers, so let me give you a thirty-thousand-foot view of some of the standout moments.

- **EXODUS.** After Joseph died, a generation of Egyptians forgot about his contributions and his leadership. They began to mistreat the Israelites. The Egyptian pharaoh enslaved God's people and oppressed them harshly. But God heard the cry of his people and raised up a new leader to free them from slavery: Moses. Moses led the Israelites out of Egyptian slavery and into the Desert of Sinai so that they could worship God freely, but not before Moses had to deal with some major insecurities. Not only did Moses recommend to God that he choose a different leader, but he also questioned God's choice several times.

  Moses' insecurities show us on a micro level what happened with the Israelites in the desert: They doubted God. What became clear about Israel's time in the Desert of Sinai is that God would faithfully meet all their needs and accompany them with his staying presence. But despite their newfound freedom, the miraculous signs and wonders God displayed before them, and God's tender provision and care, the Israelites rebelled against God time and time again in the desert.

- **LEVITICUS.** While the Israelites were in the wilderness on their way to the Promised Land, God commemorated his covenant with the Ten Commandments and outlined a flourishing life that he would sustain. How would the people enjoy God's commitment to them? Obedience. God knew the best way for his people to experience his goodness, but the Israelites rejected God and his way of living. Which brings us to the book of Numbers.

- **NUMBERS.** The book of Numbers details the last days the Israelites spent in the Sinai Desert. Numbers was written to a specific original audience: the Israelites about to enter the Promised Land. Sadly, the Israelites' insecurities got the best of them, and they experienced a series of conflicts that demonstrated their failure to believe that God is good. That's what insecurity does, isn't it? It pulls on a little thread of doubt before our faith comes unraveled. It's a nagging voice in our head that whispers *He's going to let the shoe drop.*

The Israelites' insecurities are cringey and oh-so-relatable. The stories we are going to explore together give us a heart-level view of how to become lost in a desert you were destined to get through. In all three rebellion stories, you're going to see what it looks like to settle somewhere you were only intended to make a pit stop.

If you've ever sensed that your life is in a holding pattern or that you're stuck in liminal space, this lesson is for you. Our in-between places tend to reveal our capacity for faith. Are we prone to wander, feeling lost? Or can we be the kind of Christ followers who stay in step with him to enjoy our foundness in God? You've heard it said that "time will tell," but what I want to submit to you is that "the place will tell." The Desert of Sinai is a place that represents our insecurities. A place where our lack of trust trips us up—and, as the Israelites show us, prohibits us from enjoying the fullness of God's blessings.

The Israelites' biggest challenge is not, as we might expect, marauding bands or lack of food and water or scorpions or blazing sun. The single greatest threat to their survival in the wilderness is themselves. They are enemy #1. It's enough to make Moses wish he were dead. Literally.[1]

Carmen Joy Imes, *Bearing God's Name*

---

1. **PERSONAL CONTEXT: What is going on in your life right now that might impact how you understand the Desert of Sinai story? What do you hope to learn from this lesson?**

2. **SPIRITUAL CONTEXT: If you've never studied the Desert of Sinai before, what piques your curiosity? If you've studied this place before, what impressions and insights do you recall?**

3. **BIBLICAL CONTEXT: What questions come to mind as you read about the context of the wilderness wanderings? What questions do you wish you could have answered before studying this part of Scripture?**

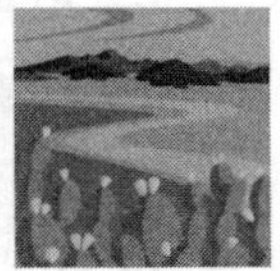

SEEING

Seeing the text is vital if we want the heart of the Scripture passage to sink in. We read slowly and intentionally through the text with the context in mind. As we practice close, thoughtful reading of Scripture, we pick up on phrases, implications, and meanings we might otherwise have missed. Part 2 includes close Scripture reading and observation questions to empower you to answer the question *What is the story saying?*

1. **Read about Rebellion #1 in Numbers 11:1-17. Underline anything "the people" are doing in these verses.**

11 Now when the people complained in the hearing of the LORD about their misfortunes, the LORD heard it and his anger was kindled. Then the fire of the LORD burned against them, and consumed some outlying parts of the camp. ² But the people cried out to Moses; and Moses prayed to the LORD, and the fire abated. ³ So that place was called Taberah, because the fire of the LORD burned against them.

⁴ The rabble among them had a strong craving; and the Israelites also wept again, and said, "If only we had meat to eat! ⁵ We remember the fish we used to eat in Egypt for nothing, the cucumbers, the melons, the leeks, the onions, and the garlic; ⁶ but now our strength is dried up, and there is nothing at all but this manna to look at."

[7] Now the manna was like coriander seed, and its color was like the color of gum resin. [8] The people went around and gathered it, ground it in mills or beat it in mortars, then boiled it in pots and made cakes of it; and the taste of it was like the taste of cakes baked with oil. [9] When the dew fell on the camp in the night, the manna would fall with it.

[10] Moses heard the people weeping throughout their families, all at the entrances of their tents. Then the LORD became very angry, and Moses was displeased. [11] So Moses said to the LORD, "Why have you treated your servant so badly? Why have I not found favor in your sight, that you lay the burden of all this people on me? [12] Did I conceive all this people? Did I give birth to them, that you should say to me, 'Carry them in your bosom, as a nurse carries a sucking child,' to the land that you promised on oath to their ancestors? [13] Where am I to get meat to give to all this people? For they come weeping to me and say, 'Give us meat to eat!' [14] I am not able to carry all this people alone, for they are too heavy for me. [15] If this is the way you are going to treat me, put me to death at once—if I have found favor in your sight—and do not let me see my misery."

[16] So the LORD said to Moses, "Gather for me seventy of the elders of Israel, whom you know to be the elders of the people and officers over them; bring them to the tent of meeting, and have them take their place there with you. [17] I will come down and talk with you there; and I will take some of the spirit that is on you and put it on them; and they shall bear the burden of the people along with you so that you will not bear it all by yourself."

NUMBERS 11:1-17

2. What "misfortunes" (Numbers 11:1) were the people complaining about to Moses?

3. **How did God feel about the people's grumbling? Why do you think he responded the way he did?**

4. **Summarize Numbers 11:4-6 in your own words, as if you were saying this to your best friend.**

5. **Moses asked the Lord several questions. Which question resonates most with you, and why?**

Moses asking God to put him to death is rather extreme. Moses must have been depleted and near burnout to react with such a drastic request of God. Leadership will do that to you. It will stretch you so thin you feel as though you will snap. Being fed up with the relentless burden of caring for millions of unhappy people prompted Moses to pray a really honest prayer. If you are a leader, be encouraged: You are not the only person who's ever felt like giving up after an encounter with disgruntled people. And for those of us with a propensity to see the glass half empty—who, like the Israelites, resist joy and find the downside to almost anything—let's take care not to weigh down ourselves or the people shepherding us.

Sadly, this rebellion against Moses' leadership was just the beginning of a series of ongoing grumblings among God's people. With hindsight, we see in the book of Numbers that what starts out as the people's complaining against Moses grows into a rebellion against all their leaders and ultimately causes them to turn on each other and God.

After God provides a solution to Moses' leadership crisis—commissioning more elders to serve the people—Moses sends twelve spies into the Promised Land to scout out their inheritance from the Lord. At this point in time, God's people had experienced

+ God's powerful miracles in Egypt;
+ God's liberation of them from Egyptian slavery;
+ God's staying presence, in a cloud by day and fire by night, as they trekked through the Sinai Desert;
+ God's covenant of love through the giving of the law at Mount Sinai; and
+ God's daily provision of manna and quail in the wilderness . . .
+ . . . to name a few things.

Point being: The people of Israel knew God's character. They knew his love, his faithfulness, his promises—and still they struggled to believe that he would stay true to his word. Of the twelve scouts Moses sent, only two, Caleb and Joshua, came back with a praise report. I'm paraphrasing here, but Caleb's response to their survey of the land was essentially "Let's go get what God has promised us. God will overcome the Canaanites." But the other ten spies focused on the giants occupying the land and the fortified cities. Their response was something like "Nope. They are stronger than we are." When the Israelites should have focused on God's power and his fulfilled promises of the past, they were zeroed in on the obstacles they would face along the way. Here's what happened next.

6. **Read about Rebellion #2 in Numbers 14:1–25. Circle anything you learn about God's character.**

14 Then all the congregation raised a loud cry, and the people wept that night. [2] And all the Israelites complained against Moses and Aaron; the whole congregation said to them, "Would that we had died in the land of Egypt! Or would that we had died in this wilderness! [3] Why is the LORD bringing us into this land to fall by the sword? Our wives and our little ones will become booty; would it not be better for us to go back to Egypt?" [4] So they said to one another, "Let us choose a captain, and go back to Egypt."

[5] Then Moses and Aaron fell on their faces before all the assembly of the congregation of the Israelites. [6] And Joshua son of Nun and Caleb son of Jephunneh, who were among those who had spied out the land, tore their clothes [7] and said to all the congregation of the Israelites, "The land that we went through as spies is an exceedingly good land. [8] If the LORD is pleased with us, he will bring us into this land and give it to us, a land that flows with milk and honey. [9] Only, do not rebel against the LORD; and do not fear the people of the land, for they are no more than bread for us; their protection is removed from them, and the LORD is with us; do not fear them." [10] But the whole congregation threatened to stone them.

Then the glory of the LORD appeared at the tent of meeting to all the Israelites. [11] And the LORD said to Moses, "How long will this people despise me? And how long will they refuse to believe in me, in spite of all the signs that I have done among them? [12] I will strike them with pestilence and disinherit them, and I will make of you a nation greater and mightier than they."

[13] But Moses said to the LORD, "Then the Egyptians will hear of it, for in your might you brought up this people from among them, [14] and they will tell the inhabitants of this land. They have heard that you, O LORD, are in the midst of this people; for you, O LORD, are seen face to face, and your cloud stands over them and you go in front of them, in a pillar of

cloud by day and in a pillar of fire by night. ¹⁵ Now if you kill this people all at one time, then the nations who have heard about you will say, ¹⁶ 'It is because the LORD was not able to bring this people into the land he swore to give them that he has slaughtered them in the wilderness.' ¹⁷ And now, therefore, let the power of the LORD be great in the way that you promised when you spoke, saying,

¹⁸ 'The LORD is slow to anger,
and abounding in steadfast love,
forgiving iniquity and transgression,
but by no means clearing the guilty,
visiting the iniquity of the parents
upon the children
to the third and the fourth generation.'

¹⁹ Forgive the iniquity of this people according to the greatness of your steadfast love, just as you have pardoned this people, from Egypt even until now."

²⁰ Then the LORD said, "I do forgive, just as you have asked; ²¹ nevertheless—as I live, and as all the earth shall be filled with the glory of the LORD— ²² none of the people who have seen my glory and the signs that I did in Egypt and in the wilderness, and yet have tested me these ten times and have not obeyed my voice, ²³ shall see the land that I swore to give to their ancestors; none of those who despised me shall see it. ²⁴ But my servant Caleb, because he has a different spirit and has followed me wholeheartedly, I will bring into the land into which he went, and his descendants shall possess it. ²⁵ Now, since the Amalekites and the Canaanites live in the valleys, turn tomorrow and set out for the wilderness by the way to the Red Sea."

NUMBERS 14:1-25

7. What were the people complaining about to Moses and Aaron?

8. Write out the first question in Numbers 14:3 below:

9. Based on Numbers 14:11, how did God feel about the people's rebellion? Why do you think he responded the way he did?

10. What did Moses ask the Lord to do? Why did Moses respond this way?

11. **Based on Numbers 14:20-23, what was the Lord's two-part response to Moses' request?**

Part 1:

Part 2:

12. **Based on Numbers 14:25, what body of water were they headed toward? Why would this body of water have meaning for the Israelites? What meaning do you think the Lord was evoking with the location?**

God blessed the defiant Israelites with forgiveness and also allowed them to suffer a natural consequence of their actions. Did you notice that the Lord waited for his people to reject him ten times before he allowed them to experience the consequences of their sin? You and I might want to read a harshness into God's voice here when in fact God is reminding us, again, that he is merciful and slow to anger.

Maybe you need to hear that today. God is merciful and wants to show you mercy. When you're wandering in a desert of insecurity and rebellion, God is slow to anger and doesn't want you to experience the full impact of your sinful choices.

UNDERSTANDING

Now that we've finished a close reading of the Scriptures, we're going to spend some time on interpretation: doing our best to understand what God was saying to the original audience and what he's teaching us through the process. But to do so, we need to learn his ways and consider how God's Word would have been understood by the original audience before applying the same truths to our own lives. "Scripture interpretation" may sound a little stuffy, but understanding what God means to communicate to us in the Bible is crucial to enjoying a close relationship with Jesus. Part 3 will enable you to answer the question *What does it mean?*

1. Reread about Rebellion #1 in Numbers 11:1–17. Circle every time Moses is mentioned.

11 Now when the people complained in the hearing of the LORD about their misfortunes, the LORD heard it and his anger was kindled. Then the fire of the LORD burned against them, and consumed some outlying parts of the camp. ² But the people cried out to Moses; and Moses prayed to the LORD, and the fire abated. ³ So that place was called Taberah, because the fire of the LORD burned against them.

⁴ The rabble among them had a strong craving; and the Israelites also wept again, and said, "If only we had meat to eat! ⁵ We remember the

fish we used to eat in Egypt for nothing, the cucumbers, the melons, the leeks, the onions, and the garlic; 6 but now our strength is dried up, and there is nothing at all but this manna to look at."

7 Now the manna was like coriander seed, and its color was like the color of gum resin. 8 The people went around and gathered it, ground it in mills or beat it in mortars, then boiled it in pots and made cakes of it; and the taste of it was like the taste of cakes baked with oil. 9 When the dew fell on the camp in the night, the manna would fall with it.

10 Moses heard the people weeping throughout their families, all at the entrances of their tents. Then the LORD became very angry, and Moses was displeased. 11 So Moses said to the LORD, "Why have you treated your servant so badly? Why have I not found favor in your sight, that you lay the burden of all this people on me? 12 Did I conceive all this people? Did I give birth to them, that you should say to me, 'Carry them in your bosom, as a nurse carries a sucking child,' to the land that you promised on oath to their ancestors? 13 Where am I to get meat to give to all this people? For they come weeping to me and say, 'Give us meat to eat!' 14 I am not able to carry all this people alone, for they are too heavy for me. 15 If this is the way you are going to treat me, put me to death at once—if I have found favor in your sight—and do not let me see my misery."

16 So the LORD said to Moses, "Gather for me seventy of the elders of Israel, whom you know to be the elders of the people and officers over them; bring them to the tent of meeting, and have them take their place there with you. 17 I will come down and talk with you there; and I will take some of the spirit that is on you and put it on them; and they shall bear the burden of the people along with you so that you will not bear it all by yourself."

NUMBERS 11:1-17

2. Why do you think God included the account of this rebellion in the Bible? How would it be instructive for the generation of Israelites moving into the Promised Land?

3. Are you facing any leadership challenges at home or at work? Or working through any places of insecurity in your life? Identify what's burdening you most and then write a prayer asking God to step in and help.

4. The Israelites were rebelling against the Lord's provision and the godly leadership he had appointed. Do you see this tendency anywhere in your own life? In the wider church today?

5. Based on Numbers 11:16-17, what was the Lord's solution to Moses' challenge?

6. Why would the Lord's solution in Numbers 11 be instructive to the Israelites who were going to live in the Promised Land?

7. How should the Lord's solution challenge us today? Is the Holy Spirit bringing to mind a specific burden you're carrying that you need to share with others?

8. Write out the last eight words of Numbers 11:17:

9. **Reread about Rebellion #2 in Numbers 14:1-25. In the margin, list anything you learn about the Lord from this passage.**

14 Then all the congregation raised a loud cry, and the people wept that night. 2 And all the Israelites complained against Moses and Aaron; the whole congregation said to them, "Would that we had died in the land of Egypt! Or would that we had died in this wilderness! 3 Why is the LORD bringing us into this land to fall by the sword? Our wives and our little ones will become booty; would it not be better for us to go back to Egypt?" 4 So they said to one another, "Let us choose a captain, and go back to Egypt."

5 Then Moses and Aaron fell on their faces before all the assembly of the congregation of the Israelites. 6 And Joshua son of Nun and Caleb son of Jephunneh, who were among those who had spied out the land, tore their clothes 7 and said to all the congregation of the Israelites, "The land that we went through as spies is an exceedingly good land. 8 If the LORD is pleased with us, he will bring us into this land and give it to us, a land that flows with milk and honey. 9 Only, do not rebel against the LORD; and do not fear the people of the land, for they are no more than bread for us; their protection is removed from them, and the LORD is with us; do not fear them." 10 But the whole congregation threatened to stone them.

Then the glory of the LORD appeared at the tent of meeting to all the Israelites. 11 And the LORD said to Moses, "How long will this people despise me? And how long will they refuse to believe in me, in spite of all the signs that I have done among them? 12 I will strike them with pestilence and disinherit them, and I will make of you a nation greater and mightier than they."

13 But Moses said to the LORD, "Then the Egyptians will hear of it, for in your might you brought up this people from among them, 14 and they will tell the inhabitants of this land. They have heard that you, O LORD, are in the midst of this people; for you, O LORD, are seen face to face, and

your cloud stands over them and you go in front of them, in a pillar of cloud by day and in a pillar of fire by night. ¹⁵ Now if you kill this people all at one time, then the nations who have heard about you will say, ¹⁶ 'It is because the LORD was not able to bring this people into the land he swore to give them that he has slaughtered them in the wilderness.' ¹⁷ And now, therefore, let the power of the LORD be great in the way that you promised when you spoke, saying,

¹⁸ 'The LORD is slow to anger,
and abounding in steadfast love,
forgiving iniquity and transgression,
but by no means clearing the guilty,
visiting the iniquity of the parents
upon the children
to the third and the fourth generation.'

¹⁹ Forgive the iniquity of this people according to the greatness of your steadfast love, just as you have pardoned this people, from Egypt even until now."

²⁰ Then the LORD said, "I do forgive, just as you have asked; ²¹ nevertheless—as I live, and as all the earth shall be filled with the glory of the LORD— ²² none of the people who have seen my glory and the signs that I did in Egypt and in the wilderness, and yet have tested me these ten times and have not obeyed my voice, ²³ shall see the land that I swore to give to their ancestors; none of those who despised me shall see it. ²⁴ But my servant Caleb, because he has a different spirit and has followed me wholeheartedly, I will bring into the land into which he went, and his descendants shall possess it. ²⁵ Now, since the Amalekites and the Canaanites live in the valleys, turn tomorrow and set out for the wilderness by the way to the Red Sea."

NUMBERS 14:1-25

10. How would the Israelites about to enter the Promised Land be impacted by these stories that Moses wrote? Why would they need these stories to inform their faith for the future?

11. Describe the last time you disobeyed God. What was going on internally and externally when you rejected God or his ways?

12. What consequences have you experienced as a result of not caring about God's instructions?

13. What grace have you experienced because of God's forgiveness?

If you only knew how much I need God's mercy in my life. I am sick over some behaviors in my past and feel weighed down with regret. Not only am I suffering the consequences of my choices, but so are some of the people I love.

That's why I, for one, am overwhelmed with gratitude that God forgave the people who didn't get to see the Promised Land. Not enjoying their inheritance was a terrible outcome, but it could have been much worse. God could have given them what they deserved. Instead, he acted in line with his character—with abounding love.

However you are processing this story, I want to remind you that it's not too late to ask for forgiveness. It's not too late to confess your sin. It's never too late to find God's embrace again. He's drawing you in close to cover your sins with his love.

In this description of the Israelites in the wilderness, Numbers gives us a detailed picture of human weakness. We see dissatisfaction and greed. We see jealousy and rivalry. We see malicious gossip and back-stairs plots. We see ingratitude, selfishness, and stupidity. In short, we see the kinds of things that go on wherever groups of human beings are gathered together.[2]

Fleming Rutledge, *And God Spoke to Abraham*

An important part of understanding the meaning of a Bible passage is getting a sense of its place in the broader storyline of Scripture. When we make connections between different parts of the Bible, we get a glimpse of the unity and cohesion of the Scriptures.

The Desert of Sinai shows us the wanderings of rebellion, but in the book of Deuteronomy, Moses demonstrates that rebellion is never the end of the story because God is with us in every desert.

14. Read Moses' final speech to the Israelites as he describes a vivid picture of belonging to God despite our rebellion toward him in Deuteronomy 1:26-33. Underline what Moses says about God carrying his people.

26 But you were unwilling to go up. You rebelled against the command of the LORD your God; 27 you grumbled in your tents and said, "It is because the LORD hates us that he has brought us out of the land of Egypt, to hand us over to the Amorites to destroy us. 28 Where are we headed? Our kindred have made our hearts melt by reporting, 'The people are stronger and taller than we; the cities are large and fortified up to heaven! We actually saw there the offspring of the Anakim!'" 29 I said to you, "Have no dread or fear of them. 30 The LORD your God, who goes before you, is the one who will fight for you, just as he did for you in Egypt before your very eyes, 31 and in the wilderness, where you saw how the LORD your God carried you, just as one carries a child, all the way that you traveled until you reached this place. 32 But in spite of this, you have no trust in the LORD your God, 33 who goes before you on the way to seek out a place for you to camp, in fire by night, and in the cloud by day, to show you the route you should take."

DEUTERONOMY 1:26-33

15. Using the list below, match the insecurities with a verse in Deuteronomy 1:26-33.

(Example: __26__ The insecurity of leaving home to get to the Promised Land.)

The Israelites' Insecurities

___ The insecurity of believing that God's commands aren't worth it.
___ The insecurity of believing that others have it better than you.
___ The insecurity of believing that the Lord hates you.
___ The insecurity of believing that the Lord intends to destroy you.
___ The insecurity of feeling small, insignificant, and weak.
___ The insecurity of believing that new places will not be welcoming.
___ The insecurity of focusing on what you can see and not living by faith.
___ The insecurity of dread.
___ The insecurity of fear.
___ The insecurity of not trusting the Lord.

16. Circle any of the insecurities listed above that you're struggling with right now. Which undermines your faith the most? Which causes you to feel distant from God?

17. Based on Deuteronomy 1:31, how does God carry you?

18. How does that image of God encourage and comfort you?

Like a mother or father carrying their beloved child, God is carrying you. God is on your side, just as he was for the Israelites. He's making a way through, he's been by your side the whole way, and he's meeting all your needs. And he always will.

Although the list of the Israelites' insecurities is long, so is the list of all the truths we learn about God's relationship with the Israelites.

Truths about God in the Desert
+ The Lord is God.
+ The Lord goes before you.
+ The Lord will fight for you.
+ The Lord will defeat your enemies.
+ The Lord will set you free from slavery.
+ The Lord will carry you through the desert.
+ The Lord will be by your side all the way to the end.
+ The Lord will show you the route to take.

+ + +

Let's check back in on our Deserts Storyline.

THE DESERTS STORYLINE OF SCRIPTURE

Location	Words from God for Desert Seasons	On the Other Side of the Desert
The Deserts of Shur and Beersheba (Genesis 16, 21)	[The angel of the LORD said,] "Where have you come from and where are you going?" (Genesis 16:8) [The angel of God said,] "What troubles you?" (Genesis 21:17)	Hagar went through rejection to get to protection.
The Desert of Dothan (Genesis 37, 45, 50)	[Joseph said,] "Do not be afraid! Am I in the place of God? Even though you intended to do harm to me, God intended it for good." (Genesis 50:19-20)	Joseph's brothers went through resentment to get to forgiveness.
The Desert of Sinai (Numbers 11, 14)	[The LORD said,] "How long will this people despise me? And how long will they refuse to believe in me, in spite of all the signs that I have done among them?" (Numbers 14:11)	The Israelites went through insecurity to get to belonging.
The Desert of Judea (Matthew 3–4)	[Jesus said,] "It is written, 'Do not put the Lord your God to the test.'" (Matthew 4:7)	Jesus went through trials to get to ministry.
The Deserts of Ministry (Matthew 14, 15)	[Jesus asked,] "How many loaves have you?" (Matthew 15:34)	The disciples went through scarcity to get to abundance.

1. **What about the Desert of Sinai story resonates with you most? What part of the story piques your curiosity?**

2. **What did you learn about God in this lesson? And what did you learn about yourself in this lesson?**

3. **How should these truths shape your faith community and change you?**

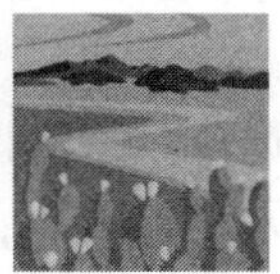

RESPONDING

The purpose of Bible study is to help you become more Christlike; that's why part 4 will include journaling space for your reflection on and responses to the content and a blank checklist for actionable next steps. You'll be able to process what you're learning so that you can live out the concepts and pursue Christlikeness. Part 4 will enable you to answer the questions *What truths is this passage teaching?* and *How do I apply this to my life?*

WHAT'S HELD MY ATTENTION through the rebellions in the book of Numbers is God's purposeful use of geography. The farther away they got from Egypt—where they were enslaved—and the closer they got to freedom in the Promised Land, the more the Israelites' insecurities intensified. Instead of enjoying God's constant presence and provision through every twist and turn in their journey, they chose to resist God's goodness. And for what? Grumbling, complaining, whining, bemoaning the route God had mapped out for them.

I've found their example to be so painfully convicting that I got a pit in my stomach as I imagined how much regret filled their lives. Especially in light of the belonging God has created his people for.

If we let insecurities rule us, we won't be able to experience the full blessings of belonging to God. At the very heart of all insecurities is a sick sense that we don't belong—where we live, where we go to church, in our friend group, on this team.

Which couldn't be further from the truth. Because of God's loyal love, you always belong with and to him. Here are three truths to meditate on as you consider how to fully embrace your God-promised belonging in Christ.

1. IT'S TIME TO LET YOUR INSECURITIES DIE IN THE DESERT.

I'm prone to catastrophizing and letting my insecurities override my faith. When I find myself in a desert moment, I begin looking around and thinking, *I'm going to die here.* What I want to and could choose to focus on are thoughts like *God is with me now. I have everything I need to survive this. God is actively working on my behalf so that this will be used for my good.* To everyone stuck in the wilderness, to everyone wandering in this part of your spiritual journey, hear me: You will survive this desert. But this could also be a prime opportunity to leave your insecurities at this pit stop for good.

2. YOU BELONG IN THE PROMISED LAND.

You weren't created to live in the desert but to travel through it. This is no time to look back to Egypt and wish for slavery. You belong in the Promised Land. I'm concerned that many of us are so familiar with desert wastelands that we hardly remember who we are in Christ. We are not desert dwellers; we are promise receivers. For the original readers of the Bible—and the Israelites who physically wandered through the Desert of Sinai—the journey was a physical reminder of all the spiritual lessons they learned along the way. God provides. God is present. God meets our needs. God can be trusted. God's promises hold. Although you and I may never walk from Egypt to Israel on foot—or fear starvation, extinction, or war—we are all fighting metaphorical battles of faith. We're living through circumstances that could cause us to become more insecure—or that could lead us to a flourishing life of belonging.

3. YOU BELONG TO GOD.

My son, Caleb, is eleven as I write this study, and right now he's struggling to find a friend group at school. So much of our adolescent years is spent searching for belonging, for a group of friends you hope will claim you as "one of us."

That's why we've started greeting Caleb after school with a ten-second hug and our *you're-home!* liturgy: *You're home now. You're one of us. Always. An Armstrong forever. God's beloved son. God loves you no matter what. You are God's dream come true.* My prayer is that these words I'm speaking over Caleb will take root in his young soul. Because what I know as a middle-aged adult is that people of all ages face a lifelong battle with their identity, their belonging. When we are new to a job, new to parenting, new to a church, deep inside we are longing to answer this burning question: *Do I belong here?* There is meaning and purpose in exploring that question, but I don't want you to miss the truth that you belong to God. If God is everywhere, and I believe he is, then no matter where you are, you can enjoy a belongingness that comes with being a child of God.

Ask yourself how these truths impact your relationship with God and with others.

What is the Holy Spirit bringing to your mind as actionable next steps in your faith journey?

- ✦
- ✦
- ✦

GOING THROUGH TRIALS TO GET TO MINISTRY

THE DESERT OF JUDEA: WHERE JESUS IS TESTED

SCRIPTURE: MATTHEW 3–4

CONTEXT

Before you begin your study, we will start with the context of the story we are about to read together: the setting, both cultural and historical; the people involved; and where our passage fits in the larger setting of Scripture. All these things help us make sense of what we're reading. Understanding the context of a Bible story is fundamental to reading Scripture well. Getting your bearings before you read will enable you to answer the question *What am I about to read?*

I'M TEACHING a fourth- and fifth-grade Sunday school class, and these brilliant young theologians are the highlight of my week every week. Seeing life and reading the Bible through their eyes is shaping my own way of doing both. We start every class with the same invitation: "Tell me something good." I want to hear about their baseball games, gymnastics meets, new pet slugs, and upcoming trips to visit grandparents so that we can celebrate what God is doing in their lives.

The first week of May is different though. Show up to our Sunday school class near the end of a school year, and you'll hear guttural groans from the kids as they prepare to take end-of-year exams. The answer that week to "Tell me something good" is "Testing will be over soon!" as they melt into their chairs like ice cream.

I feel for the kids. Testing is no fun. But academic challenges can serve a beneficial purpose: They tell the truth about what we know.

You and I could have a lengthy conversation about the overuse of testing in schools and the misapplication of test results, but the point I want to make is this: Tests serve an important function both in education *and* in our spiritual development. The best teachers utilize testing to take an inventory, much like a progress report, of gaps in understanding that need attention. God does something similar with us. God allows our faith to be tested so that we can find out what we really believe about God and ourselves.

If you've been taught that God is cruel, all this talk about testing probably spooks you a bit. But God's not out to get you. God is not cruel. God is love. He's not setting traps so that he can catch and punish you. Only Satan does that.

Tests from God might make us groan like my fourth- and fifth-grade students, but the truth is that the tests God allows in your life are not to harm you but to bring good. He promises to be with you through the whole ordeal and has a supernatural way of redeeming circumstances into viewpoints of grace.

Of course, that ultimate good doesn't mean we experience the test as good. The test is a test. We don't have to bypass or ignore the pain the challenge might cause. But we can accept adversity as a natural part of our spiritual lives and enjoy trusting God to get us through the test and on to reviewing the results together. Easier said than done, right?

Trials don't determine whether you're going to pass Christianity and get into heaven. Your crucible is not a spiritual report card; it is a progress report on your faith in God. Matthew's Gospel begins with Jesus being tested, and much of the Gospel account gives the nation of Israel a progress report on their faith.

Israel had come a long way since their wanderings in the Sinai wilderness, but had they learned from their many deserts of exile and rebellion? Now, in the book of Matthew, a New Moses arrives to go through the wilderness and show his people what faithfulness to God looks like.

Matthew makes sure we know that Jesus is King. Jesus, the new King of Israel, is in the line of David, has been tested in the wilderness like Moses, and has fulfilled the Torah. King Jesus is the New Moses on the New Mountain, giving the New Law to lead the New Exodus for a New Passover. The Moses-Jesus connection links the Old Testament to the New and verifies that Jesus is who he claims to be: the Jewish Messiah.

MOSES AND JESUS COMPARED[1]

	Moses	Jesus
An Infant Survival Story	Moses survived the Egyptian pharaoh's edict to kill all the newborn Hebrew boys in Egypt (Exodus 1:1–2:10).	Jesus survived King Herod's edict to kill all the young Hebrew boys in Bethlehem (Matthew 2).
"Out of Egypt"	Moses fled Egypt after killing an Egyptian, and God called him to return once the pharaoh had died (Exodus 2:11–3:10).	God told Mary and Joseph to flee with Jesus to Egypt to protect him from Herod, and they returned once Herod had died (Matthew 2:13-15, 19-23).
Shepherds	Moses was a shepherd (Exodus 3:1).	Jesus referred to himself as the Good Shepherd (John 10:11).
A Deliverance Ministry	Moses led the Israelites out of Egyptian slavery (Exodus 12:50-51).	"Jesus also came to deliver his people, all who would trust in him, but from a much more powerful enemy: the tyranny of sin."[2]
A Cosmic Water Event	Moses witnessed God part the Red Sea and then the drowning of the pharaoh's army (Exodus 14).	Jesus was baptized in the Jordan River (Matthew 3:13-17) and offers Living Water (John 4:7-14).
Forty Units of Time in the Wilderness	Moses guided the Israelites through the desert for forty years (Numbers 32:13).	Jesus was led by the Spirit into the desert for testing after forty days of fasting (Matthew 4:1-2).
Covenant Mediation and Law Giving	Moses mediated God's Ten Commandments and the (Mosaic) covenant at Mount Sinai (Exodus 19–20).	Jesus came to fulfill the law (Matthew 5:17).

Unlike Moses and the nation of Israel, Jesus aces all his tests. Jesus knows his identity as the King of Israel, and he knows that God the Father can be trusted.

Before he enters three years of ministry on earth, Jesus is led by the Spirit into the wilderness of Judea. Matthew assumes that you and I will be familiar with several terms in the story that will impact our interpretations and applications.

+ *Satan*; *the devil*; *the tempter*: the one who tries to incite people to sin by exploiting their weaknesses
+ *Son of God*: a title for Jesus

The language of sonship in the New Testament communicates God's endorsement, commission, and empowerment of Jesus as the chosen king (Bateman, "Defining the Titles," 547). When the Gospel authors spoke of Jesus as the Son of God, they may have intended the title in the sense of the Old Testament regal notion of a divinely chosen king. For example, God's voice of approval— my "beloved son"—spoken to Jesus at His baptism (Mark 1:11) has a verbal connection with Psa 2:7 and hearkens to first-century Jewish messianic expectations and the Judaism of his time.[3]

David Seal, "Son of God," in *The Lexham Bible Dictionary*

Three of the Gospels include the account of Jesus' temptation, but none of the disciples—including those who wrote or informed the content of the Gospels—were around for Jesus' three tests in the Desert of Judea. This means that Jesus must have taught his disciples about his testing to prepare them for their own faith tests. God knew that they—and you and I—would need an example of how to bear up under hardship and maintain our trust in him.

I realize some of us might be tempted to roll our eyes at Jesus rising to the occasion. You might be thinking something like *Of course he passes these tests—he's God!* But as we study this desert, I hope you see that Jesus shows us that he is also the ultimate test key in whatever wilderness trial we find ourselves in.

What you're about to read is not a story about Jesus showing off his deity but a story about Jesus entering into our pain. A King willing to endure what we go through so that he could prove his commitment to you and me. Jesus chose to experience tests to remind us that he's in this with us. And it's a story about how the temptations of the enemy in the desert are traps, while God shows us the way to life.

1. **PERSONAL CONTEXT: What is going on in your life right now that might impact how you understand Jesus' testing in the Desert of Judea? What do you hope to learn from this lesson?**

2. **SPIRITUAL CONTEXT: If you've never studied Jesus' testing in the Desert of Judea before, what piques your curiosity? If you've studied this story or place before, what impressions and insights do you recall?**

3. **BIBLICAL CONTEXT: What questions come to mind as you read about the context of Jesus' testing? What questions do you wish you could have answered before studying this part of Scripture?**

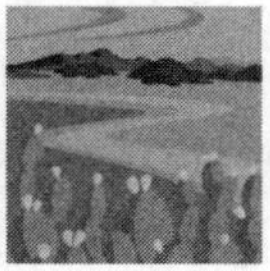

SEEING

Seeing the text is vital if we want the heart of the Scripture passage to sink in. We read slowly and intentionally through the text with the context in mind. As we practice close, thoughtful reading of Scripture, we pick up on phrases, implications, and meanings we might otherwise have missed. Part 2 includes close Scripture reading and observation questions to empower you to answer the question *What is the story saying?*

1. **Read Matthew 3. Underline any mention of the wilderness or desert.**

3 In those days John the Baptist came, preaching in the wilderness of Judea ² and saying, "Repent, for the kingdom of heaven has come near." ³ This is he who was spoken of through the prophet Isaiah:

"A voice of one calling in the wilderness,
'Prepare the way for the Lord,
    make straight paths for him.'"

⁴ John's clothes were made of camel's hair, and he had a leather belt around his waist. His food was locusts and wild honey. ⁵ People went out to him from Jerusalem and all Judea and the whole region of the Jordan. ⁶ Confessing their sins, they were baptized by him in the Jordan River.

⁷ But when he saw many of the Pharisees and Sadducees coming to where he was baptizing, he said to them: "You brood of vipers! Who warned you to flee from the coming wrath? ⁸ Produce fruit in keeping with repentance. ⁹ And do not think you can say to yourselves, 'We have Abraham as our father.' I tell you that out of these stones God can raise up children for Abraham. ¹⁰ The ax is already at the root of the trees, and every tree that does not produce good fruit will be cut down and thrown into the fire.

¹¹ "I baptize you with water for repentance. But after me comes one who is more powerful than I, whose sandals I am not worthy to carry. He will baptize you with the Holy Spirit and fire. ¹² His winnowing fork is in his hand, and he will clear his threshing floor, gathering his wheat into the barn and burning up the chaff with unquenchable fire."

¹³ Then Jesus came from Galilee to the Jordan to be baptized by John. ¹⁴ But John tried to deter him, saying, "I need to be baptized by you, and do you come to me?"

¹⁵ Jesus replied, "Let it be so now; it is proper for us to do this to fulfill all righteousness." Then John consented.

¹⁶ As soon as Jesus was baptized, he went up out of the water. At that moment heaven was opened, and he saw the Spirit of God descending like a dove and alighting on him. ¹⁷ And a voice from heaven said, "This is my Son, whom I love; with him I am well pleased."

MATTHEW 3, NIV

2. What did God's voice from heaven say about Jesus?

3. Considering the suffering Jesus would one day endure on the cross, why do you think it was important for God to call Jesus his son and say he loved him? And why was it important for Jesus to hear that he was God's beloved?

4. Why do you think it was important for God to say he was "well pleased" with Jesus? And why was it important for Jesus to hear that God was well pleased with him before his testing?

God's public declaration that Jesus is the Son of God, the King of Israel, the New Moses, came before Jesus' testing. God's announcement confirmed Jesus' identity as God, Savior, and Messiah and also emphasized the relationship Jesus has with God the Father.

5. What identity struggles are you facing right now? What identity struggles have you faced in the past?

6. What relationship struggles are you facing right now? What relationship struggles have you faced in the past?

7. How do your identity and relationship challenges impact your faith in God?

    Identity challenges:

    Relationship challenges:

8. **Read Matthew 4:1-11. Underline any mention of the wilderness or desert and circle any other locations referenced in the story.**

4 Then Jesus was led up by the Spirit into the wilderness to be tested by the devil. ² He fasted forty days and forty nights, and afterward he was famished. ³ The tempter came and said to him, "If you are the Son of God, command these stones to become loaves of bread." ⁴ But he answered, "It is written,

'One does not live by bread alone,
    but by every word that comes from the mouth of God.'"

⁵ Then the devil took him to the holy city and placed him on the pinnacle of the temple, ⁶ saying to him, "If you are the Son of God, throw yourself down, for it is written,

'He will command his angels concerning you,'
    and 'On their hands they will bear you up,
so that you will not dash your foot against a stone.'"

⁷ Jesus said to him, "Again it is written, 'Do not put the Lord your God to the test.'"
    ⁸ Again, the devil took him to a very high mountain and showed him all the kingdoms of the world and their glory, ⁹ and he said to him, "All these I will give you, if you will fall down and worship me." ¹⁰ Then Jesus said to him, "Away with you, Satan! for it is written,

'Worship the Lord your God,
    and serve only him.'"

¹¹ Then the devil left him, and suddenly angels came and waited on him.

MATTHEW 4:1-11, NRSVᵤₑ

9. Match each question with its correct answer:

Why was Jesus led to the wilderness/desert?	testing
Who led Jesus to the wilderness/desert?	fast
What did Jesus do in the wilderness/desert?	the Spirit
What was Jesus' body's response to forty days of fasting?	being famished

10. Fill in each blank in the table on the next page with one of these three options:

+ Jesus' faith in God's process
+ Jesus' faith in God's protection
+ Jesus' faith in God's provision

THE TESTING OF JESUS

The Devil's Challenge to Jesus	Jesus' Response	The Verse Jesus Quoted	The Location of the Conversation	What the Tempter Was Testing
TEST #1				
"If you are the Son of God, command these stones to become loaves of bread." (Matthew 4:3)	"It is written, 'One does not live by bread alone, but by every word that comes from the mouth of God.'" (Matthew 4:4)	"He humbled you by letting you hunger, then by feeding you . . . in order to make you understand that one does not live by bread alone, but by every word that comes from the mouth of the LORD." (Deuteronomy 8:3)	the Desert of Judea	
TEST #2				
"If you are the Son of God, throw yourself down." (Matthew 4:6)	"Again it is written, 'Do not put the Lord your God to the test.'" (Matthew 4:7)	"Do not put the LORD your God to the test, as you tested him at Massah." (Deuteronomy 6:16)	the pinnacle of the Temple in Jerusalem, the "holy city" (Matthew 4:5)	
TEST #3				
"All these I will give you, if you will fall down and worship me." (Matthew 4:9)	"Away with you, Satan! for it is written, 'Worship the Lord your God, and serve only him.'" (Matthew 4:10)	"The LORD your God you shall fear; him you shall serve, and by his name alone you shall swear." (Deuteronomy 6:13)	"a very high mountain" (Matthew 4:8)	

God's timing and God's truth both played a vital role in Jesus' response to this test. Remember, it was *after* Jesus' baptism that God allowed Jesus to be tempted so that the Scriptures would be fulfilled—after public affirmation of Jesus' role in the world and his relationship with God the Father.

11. What can we learn from this sequence of events?

As I read about Jesus' experiences in the Desert of Judea, I sensed the Holy Spirit prompting me to consider whether I am secure enough in my identity in Christ and my relationship with God to get through difficult circumstances. My answer is no. I have work to do. And I want to get to work now, before I find myself in a spiritual desert. If we don't know our identity in Christ or find security in our relationship with God, any test we face will reveal a lack of faith. Jesus was full of faith because his identity and his relationship with God were secure.

Did you notice that both the tempter and Jesus quoted God's truth? The devil manipulated Scripture to test Jesus, and Jesus used Scripture to counter the manipulation with truth. It is a sobering reminder that our enemy knows God's truth and will twist and weaponize the Scriptures against us.

Jesus doesn't just know what God's Word says; he also knows the Author and the Author's intent. Jesus knows God's heart, his mind, his will. Yes, part of this all-knowing power of Christ is because of his deity. Jesus knows what God is like because Jesus is God, united with the Father in the Holy Trinity. God the Father, God the Son, and God the Holy Spirit are three persons, one essence. But Jesus also knows God's character because he's familiar with all the books in the Old Testament. Genesis through Malachi bring sharp focus to God's purpose for his people, his tenderness toward our needs, his loyalty and love despite our constant rebellion.

You and I don't need omniscience to interpret God's Word; we need to study and absorb God's Word in a way that empowers us not only to quote verses but also to have full confidence in God's intent. Simply knowing what God's Word says is not the goal—it is the means to the goal: knowing Christ and becoming more like him.

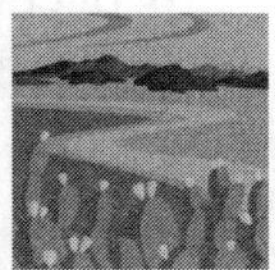

UNDERSTANDING

Now that we've finished a close reading of the Scriptures, we're going to spend some time on interpretation: doing our best to understand what God was saying to the original audience and what he's teaching us through the process. But to do so, we need to learn his ways and consider how God's Word would have been understood by the original audience before applying the same truths to our own lives. "Scripture interpretation" may sound a little stuffy, but understanding what God means to communicate to us in the Bible is crucial to enjoying a close relationship with Jesus. Part 3 will enable you to answer the question *What does it mean?*

WHEN HE TELLS THE STORY, Matthew draws attention to the fact that Jesus' testing took place in the Desert of Judea. He wants to remind Bible readers of the harrowing journey the Israelites had experienced in the Desert of Sinai. It is almost as if Matthew wanted those reading his Gospel to imagine that they are back in the wilderness wanderings of Exodus, Leviticus, Numbers, and Deuteronomy—and that Jesus is meeting his people back where many of them left off: in the desert.

The Israelites' story in the wilderness is so relatable, isn't it? We can so often find ourselves wandering through our own spiritual and circumstantial deserts. Although we may not experience the physical dangers of the Israelites' life in the wilderness, we are all facing our own battles and fighting off temptation in our metaphorical wastelands.

What was true for the Israelites is true for us: If we don't know who we are and whose we are, difficult circumstances will tempt us to mistrust ourselves and God.

That's why the devil was trying to deceive Jesus in the desert. The devil wanted to capitalize on Jesus' circumstances. The deceiver knew that any chance to undermine Jesus' identity as God's Son, and his inseparable relationship with God, would be most effective in the desert—where God's people are most vulnerable.

Three times Satan tried to attack Jesus' confidence in God with a pointed observation: Jesus' circumstances didn't seem to reflect that God can be trusted. But to judge God's intentions based on our circumstances is foolish. Our faith—not our circumstances—should determine our trust in God. Our faith relies on God's love-filled provision, protection, and process.

1. **Fill in each blank in the table on the next page with one of these three options:**

- skip the process
- provide for yourself
- protect yourself

IDENTIFYING YOUR OWN TESTS

The Devil's Challenge to Jesus	Jesus' Response	The Verse Jesus Quoted	The Location of the Conversation	What the Tempter Was Testing	Your Test
TEST #1					
"If you are the Son of God, command these stones to become loaves of bread." (Matthew 4:3)	"It is written, 'One does not live by bread alone, but by every word that comes from the mouth of God.'" (Matthew 4:4)	"He humbled you by letting you hunger, then by feeding you . . . in order to make you understand that one does not live by bread alone, but by every word that comes from the mouth of the LORD." (Deuteronomy 8:3)	the Desert of Judea	Jesus' faith in God's provision	
TEST #2					
"If you are the Son of God, throw yourself down." (Matthew 4:6)	"Again it is written, 'Do not put the Lord your God to the test.'" (Matthew 4:7)	"Do not put the LORD your God to the test, as you tested him at Massah." (Deuteronomy 6:16)	the pinnacle of the Temple in Jerusalem, the "holy city" (Matthew 4:5)	Jesus' faith in God's protection	
TEST #3					
"All these I will give you, if you will fall down and worship me." (Matthew 4:9)	"Away with you, Satan! for it is written, 'Worship the Lord your God, and serve only him.'" (Matthew 4:10)	"The LORD your God you shall fear; him you shall serve, and by his name alone you shall swear." (Deuteronomy 6:13)	"a very high mountain" (Matthew 4:8)	Jesus' faith in God's process	

TEST #1: PROVIDE FOR YOURSELF

When your circumstances are challenging, pay attention to your propensity to try to provide for your own needs. Of course you bear responsibilities in life to be a responsible person, but God is the One meeting your needs. After forty days of fasting, Jesus was famished. Like those of the droves of people in the Old Testament impacted by famine, Jesus' hunger pangs made him dependent upon God for daily provision of energy and strength, which God supplied. You can count on God to do the same for you.

2. In what unhealthy ways do you try to provide for yourself?

3. In which area of your life do you need God to provide for you?

4. What would it look like to trust that God will provide what you need?

TEST #2: PROTECT YOURSELF

The enemy tested Jesus' trust in God's protection by asking him to harm himself. God doesn't want you to intentionally harm yourself, and he will never ask you to do so. You can count on God to protect you, and you don't need to test him to find out whether he will.

5. In what unhealthy ways do you try to protect yourself?

6. In which area of your life do you need God to protect you?

7. What would it look like to trust that God will protect you?

TEST #3: SKIP THE PROCESS

Underneath Satan's final test for Jesus was a question: *What kind of King would Jesus be?* Would he be the kind of King who would choose power first, ascending to the throne and inheriting his Kingdom without the sacrifice of the Cross?

Or would King Jesus wait on God's timing and trust God's process? When some kings assume thrones, they try to destabilize governments, occupy the land of their enemies, plunder the possessions of their enemies, and exert their power through fear. Not Jesus. King Jesus went through the self-sacrificing process of the Crucifixion to accomplish his will. Jesus didn't grab power; he offered his life in exchange for ours.

8. In what unhealthy ways are you trying to skip the process God has created for you?

9. In which area of your life do you need to trust God's process?

10. What would it look like to trust the process God has created for you?

Take comfort in knowing that Jesus is out in front of our problems. He's ahead of you on your path, and he's ahead of me on mine. That's what we need, isn't it? Someone we can trust, someone who understands, and someone who has overcome.

11. **Read Hebrews 4:14-16. Underline every action connected to Jesus.**

14 Since, then, we have a great high priest who has passed through
the heavens, Jesus, the Son of God, let us hold fast to our confession.
15 For we do not have a high priest who is unable to sympathize with
our weaknesses, but we have one who in every respect has been tested
as we are, yet without sin. 16 Let us therefore approach the throne of
grace with boldness, so that we may receive mercy and find grace
to help in time of need.

HEBREWS 4:14-16

12. **What title does the author of Hebrews give to Jesus?**

13. **What does the author of Hebrews say is true about Jesus?**

14. **How should we respond to Jesus and his experiences?**

15. **Given what we've studied so far, why do you think the story of Jesus' testing in the
Desert of Judea would have been meaningful and encouraging to first-century
readers?**

16. **How does Jesus' testing in the Desert of Judea encourage you?**

Every time Jesus quoted Scripture during his three tests in the Desert of Judea, he quoted a Bible verse from the book of Deuteronomy.

17. Read Deuteronomy 8:2. Circle the word *testing*.

² Remember the long way that the LORD your God has led you these forty years in the wilderness, in order to humble you, testing you to know what was in your heart, whether or not you would keep his commandments.

DEUTERONOMY 8:2

18. According to Deuteronomy 8:2, why did God test the Israelites in the desert?

Let's look at Jesus' responses to Satan's tests in turn.

JESUS' RESPONSE TO THE FIRST TEST

The Devil's Challenge to Jesus	Jesus' Response	The Verse Jesus Quoted
"If you are the Son of God, command these stones to become loaves of bread." (Matthew 4:3)	"It is written, 'One does not live by bread alone, but by every word that comes from the mouth of God.'" (Matthew 4:4)	"He humbled you by letting you hunger, then by feeding you . . . in order to make you understand that one does not live by bread alone, but by every word that comes from the mouth of the LORD." (Deuteronomy 8:3)

19. Why do you think Jesus quoted Deuteronomy 8:3?

JESUS' RESPONSE TO THE SECOND TEST

The Devil's Challenge to Jesus	Jesus' Response	The Verse Jesus Quoted
"If you are the Son of God, throw yourself down." (Matthew 4:6)	"Again it is written, 'Do not put the Lord your God to the test.'" (Matthew 4:7)	"Do not put the LORD your God to the test, as you tested him at Massah." (Deuteronomy 6:16)

20. Why do you think Jesus quoted Deuteronomy 6:16?

JESUS' RESPONSE TO THE THIRD TEST

The Devil's Challenge to Jesus	Jesus' Response	The Verse Jesus Quoted
"All these I will give you, if you will fall down and worship me." (Matthew 4:9)	"Away with you, Satan! for it is written, 'Worship the Lord your God, and serve only him.'" (Matthew 4:10)	"The LORD your God you shall fear; him you shall serve, and by his name alone you shall swear." (Deuteronomy 6:13)

21. Why do you think Jesus quoted Deuteronomy 6:13?

22. Read Deuteronomy 8:14-16. Underline any reference to the wilderness or desert.

¹⁴ Do not exalt yourself, forgetting the LORD your God, who brought you out of the land of Egypt, out of the house of slavery, ¹⁵ who led you through the great and terrible wilderness, an arid wasteland with poisonous snakes and scorpions. He made water flow for you from flint rock, ¹⁶ and fed you in the wilderness with manna that your ancestors did not know, to humble you and to test you, and in the end to do you good.

DEUTERONOMY 8:14-16

23. Based on Deuteronomy 8:14-16, what was God ultimately trying to accomplish in the Israelites through the tests they experienced in the wilderness?

24. What good could come from the testing you are living through right now?

* * *

Let's check back in on our Deserts Storyline.

THE DESERTS STORYLINE OF SCRIPTURE

Location	Words from God for Desert Seasons	On the Other Side of the Desert
The Deserts of Shur and Beersheba (Genesis 16, 21)	[The angel of the LORD said,] "Where have you come from and where are you going?" (Genesis 16:8) [The angel of God said,] "What troubles you?" (Genesis 21:17)	Hagar went through rejection to get to protection.
The Desert of Dothan (Genesis 37, 45, 50)	[Joseph said,] "Do not be afraid! Am I in the place of God? Even though you intended to do harm to me, God intended it for good." (Genesis 50:19–20)	Joseph's brothers went through resentment to get to forgiveness.
The Desert of Sinai (Numbers 11, 14)	[The LORD said,] "How long will this people despise me? And how long will they refuse to believe in me, in spite of all the signs that I have done among them?" (Numbers 14:11)	The Israelites went through insecurity to get to belonging.
The Desert of Judea (Matthew 3–4)	[Jesus said,] "It is written, 'Do not put the Lord your God to the test.'" (Matthew 4:7)	Jesus went through trials to get to ministry.
The Deserts of Ministry (Matthew 14, 15)	[Jesus asked,] "How many loaves have you?" (Matthew 15:34)	The disciples went through scarcity to get to abundance.

1. **What about the Desert of Judea story resonates with you most? What part of the story piques your curiosity?**

2. **What did you learn about God in this lesson? And what did you learn about yourself in this lesson?**

3. **How should these truths shape your faith community and change you?**

RESPONDING

The purpose of Bible study is to help you become more Christlike; that's why part 4 will include journaling space for your reflection on and responses to the content and a blank checklist for actionable next steps. You'll be able to process what you're learning so that you can live out the concepts and pursue Christlikeness. Part 4 will enable you to answer the questions *What truths is this passage teaching?* and *How do I apply this to my life?*

TESTING LEADS TO MINISTRY. I know that as soon as I say *ministry*, many will self-eliminate and want to skip to lesson five. But hear me out. When I use the term *ministry*, I do not have in mind pastors or missionaries. Being in ministry is broader than being a vocational clergyperson or a seminary scholar. Every single Christian has a ministry. However you spend your days is your ministry. For some, parenting or grandparenting is your ministry, or one of the many ways you serve God. For others, your work is your ministry. If you follow Christ, you're in ministry. As a result, whenever you work through a faith test, your contributions to God's Kingdom are amplified. Your impact grows.

Without fail, every faith test Jesus has redeemed in my life has led to new opportunities to share with others what God has accomplished. On the other side of your desert testing are *more* ministry opportunities.

Think about your own life and the most effective ministry you've done over the years. What test did you complete to impact others?

Notice with me Jesus' journey from testing to ministry.

JESUS' JOURNEY

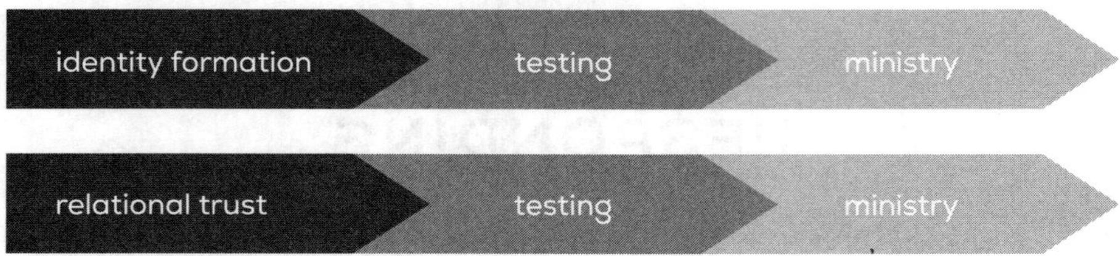

Because Jesus willingly endured several tests from Satan about his identity as the Son of God and his relationship to the Father, you and I can take heart when our own identity is challenged. Whether you are fighting internal battles of shame or external accusations that undermine your God-given identity as beloved, know this: Nothing and nobody else defines your identity.

Your identity is secure in Christ.

And if you're wrestling with loneliness, isolation, or rejection, I want to remind you that Jesus went through the same thing. The enemy tried to weaken Christ's trust in the Father by attacking the strength of their relationship. He will try the same tactic with you. Resist the devil. Refuse to succumb to Satan's attempts to make you feel less-than. Nothing and nobody determines your relationship with the Father except for Christ.

1. YOU CAN TRUST GOD'S PROVISION.

Go ahead and trust God to provide for you. Watch him give you more than you asked for or imagined. And take your answered prayers to anyone who will listen. Our world is desperate to hear that hoping in God's provision is not a fool's errand. Remind yourself and testify to others: Building lives where *we* function as our ultimate provider will leave us discouraged and overwhelmed. Life in

Christ—believing God means it when he says he will take care of us—is filled with joy and peace.

2. YOU CAN TRUST GOD'S PROTECTION.

Like he may have done for you, God once rescued me from an unhealthy friendship that could have endangered my ministry and demolished my faith. Now I can look back and see God's safety measures. Praise God for the Holy Spirit's nudging! The Lord kept throwing up red flags to warn me about codependency and deception. If you are filled with the Holy Spirit of God, listen to him. Pay attention to his warning signs.

3. YOU CAN TRUST GOD'S PROCESS.

Jesus went to the cross so that we don't have to. In so doing, Jesus proved that he would trust God's process, which would include self-sacrifice. Instead of taking his Kingdom by force, Jesus chose surrender.

Christ's willingness to suffer the Cross bewilders me. I'm actively building a life that's focused on skipping "the process." Give me all the automations that save time, create convenience, and shorten the wait. Before I start new projects or try to learn new information, I'm using a search engine to find a tutorial to create shortcuts.

While these strategies have been helpful for acquiring knowledge and creating efficiency, they have also removed resistance and friction. The kinds that produce patience, resilience, and character. Every convenience I streamline is also a temptation to resist my limits instead of checking in with the Spirit and surrendering to the process. And what do we know about the process? It is where we learn the most.

Surrender to God. Do it today. Whatever process you're trying to shortchange, give it the time and attention it deserves.

Use this journaling space to process what you are learning.

Ask yourself how these truths impact your relationship with God and with others.

What is the Holy Spirit bringing to your mind as actionable next steps in your faith journey?

✦

✦

✦

GOING THROUGH SCARCITY TO GET TO ABUNDANCE

**THE DESERTS OF MINISTRY:
WHERE JESUS FEEDS THE MULTITUDES**

SCRIPTURE: MATTHEW 14, 15

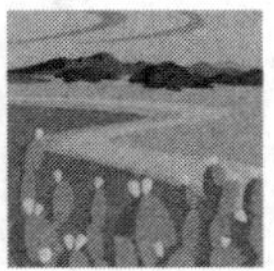

PART 1

CONTEXT

Before you begin your study, we will start with the context of the story we are about to read together: the setting, both cultural and historical; the people involved; and where our passage fits in the larger setting of Scripture. All these things help us make sense of what we're reading. Understanding the context of a Bible story is fundamental to reading Scripture well. Getting your bearings before you read will enable you to answer the question *What am I about to read?*

FOR MONTHS I had a sinking feeling in the pit of my stomach, and then it happened: My greatest fear came true. I'd been ruminating over a looming decision for so long that I'd lived through the worst-case scenario in my imagination several times over. But nothing prepares you for the moment of decision that finalizes what you've anticipated: time in a desert of disappointment and rejection. There was no way forward in my situation that wouldn't compromise what the Lord had called me to do. But not even the goal and joy of obedience removes the pain of choosing what's right, especially when what's right means letting go of a dream.

I'm a big believer in these Christian practices: speaking the possibilities of God out loud, trusting God to provide everything I need despite my lack of options, and releasing worry for God's peace and hope. But the truth is, knowing how to practice my faith and actually doing it are two different things. When I'm in a desert moment, I have to fight—and I really do mean suit up with the armor of God—to claw and swing my way out of feeling trapped and disappointed. Sadly, I am more practiced in obsessing over and rehearsing the impossibilities of desert living than in believing the God who's never left me in the desert.

I wish I could tell you that my prayer life in my most recent desert sounded something like this:

God, I have no doubt you are protecting me from something and that you will open new doors. I can't wait to see how you exceed my expectations. You love to give good gifts, and I'm waiting in hope as I trust your timing.

Instead, I muttered these phrases in my tearful, middle-of-the-night prayers for weeks before the big moment of decision:

+ *I've got nothing left.*
+ *I'm completely depleted.*
+ *My tank is empty.*
+ *I can't do this any longer.*
+ *I'm done.*

Notice the *Is* and *my* in those confessions. There's something about the wastelands and low points of life that cause Christians to turn inward instead of upward. To focus on self rather than on God. To assume we will die in the desert rather than use the desert as a way to God's abundance.

I'm not a name-it-and-claim-it Christian; the prosperity gospel gives me the heebie-jeebies. We don't manifest our realities, we are not the captains of our souls, we are not one big break away from self-actualizing a better future. We are beloved by a God who will meet all our needs richly in Christ Jesus. We are people of the promise: God will be with us always, even to the end of the age (Matthew 28:20). We are people with access to the Father through the Son and by the Spirit because of Jesus' life, death, and resurrection. We are people with a bright future because Jesus is coming back. And everything we need for life and godliness God gives us through the power of his Spirit. In the words of the psalmist, "I have what I need" (Psalm 23:1, csb).

But when I am isolated in the desert with spite in my heart because of the struggles I've had to endure, I'm prone to wander farther into the wilderness, rehearsing *Woe is me*. And yes, there's a time and place to mourn. Lament is godly. I'm not suggesting that Christians should bypass feelings, diminish our hardships, or will ourselves into finding the bright side of things. What I'm talking about is resisting despair and trusting that God provides a way out. Maybe you just need to hear that today: God is providing a way out for you.

In this lesson, we are going to study two historic moments in Jesus' ministry when the disciples were concerned about their lack of resources. Both stories happened in desertlike places. Go figure. God, storytelling genius, repurposes the familiar desert motif as the backdrop to both feeding-of-the-multitude stories in Matthew's Gospel. Keep in mind that God inspired Matthew to include not just one but two very similar stories about God providing what we need when we feel as if we have nothing. God knew you and I would need him to repeat the lesson he taught his disciples: He chooses to do his most abundant ministry work in the deserted places. Jesus brings abundance to our wilderness wanderings.

After Jesus' exit from the desert of testing (Matthew 4), he entered a season of ministry that included

+ preaching his most famous message, the Sermon on the Mount (Matthew 5–7),
+ providing life-saving healing to throngs of desperate people (Matthew 8–9),
+ deputizing his disciples with his power to preach and heal (Matthew 10), and
+ delivering profound teachings to ready the disciples for a life of service unto God (Matthew 11–13).

By all metrics, Jesus expanded his ministry. His influence grew, his following increased, and most importantly, the people he came to seek and save were flocking to him by the thousands. If you were someone eagerly waiting on life-giving words and healing touches, the exponential growth of the Jesus movement must have been a marvel to witness. But for the disciples, all they could see was lack. Which brings us to Matthew 14 and 15 and the two stories where Jesus feeds multitudes with meager handfuls of fish and bread.

This lesson is for anyone scraping the bottom of the barrel. Anyone plumb out of hope. Anyone ready to throw in the towel. This lesson is for the vigilant leader wearied by the overwhelming needs of the people you care for. And for the Christian struggling with a scarcity mindset.

You don't have enough, and I don't have enough either. But we are not alone in the desert, remember? Christ, the death-conquering, life-saving God of the universe, is right by our side, making a way through the wilderness. And just like he provided manna in the desert for the Israelites, Jesus is now, in Matthew's Gospel, proving he is the ultimate Provider. Not even a desert location will keep him from showering us, and the people we care about, with everything we need—*abundantly*.

My hope and prayer for you as you read this final lesson is that you confidently believe this: God has more for you.

1. **PERSONAL CONTEXT:** What is going on in your life right now that might impact how you understand the feedings of the multitudes in the desert? What do you hope to learn from this lesson?

2. **SPIRITUAL CONTEXT:** If you've never studied these feedings of the multitudes in the desert before, what piques your curiosity? If you've studied these stories before, what impressions and insights do you recall?

3. **BIBLICAL CONTEXT:** What questions come to mind as you read about the context of the feedings of the multitudes in the desert? What questions do you wish you could have answered before studying this part of Scripture?

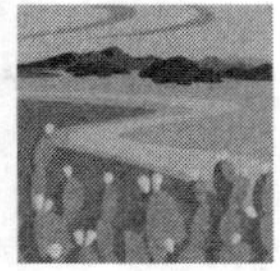

SEEING

Seeing the text is vital if we want the heart of the Scripture passage to sink in. We read slowly and intentionally through the text with the context in mind. As we practice close, thoughtful reading of Scripture, we pick up on phrases, implications, and meanings we might otherwise have missed. Part 2 includes close Scripture reading and observation questions to empower you to answer the question *What is the story saying?*

1. **Read Matthew 14:1–21. Underline everything Jesus says in the story.**

14 At that time Herod the ruler heard reports about Jesus; ² and he said to his servants, "This is John the Baptist; he has been raised from the dead, and for this reason these powers are at work in him." ³ For Herod had arrested John, bound him, and put him in prison on account of Herodias, his brother Philip's wife, ⁴ because John had been telling him, "It is not lawful for you to have her." ⁵ Though Herod wanted to put him to death, he feared the crowd, because they regarded him as a prophet. ⁶ But when Herod's birthday came, the daughter of Herodias danced before the company, and she pleased Herod ⁷ so much that he promised on oath to grant her whatever she might ask. ⁸ Prompted by her mother, she said, "Give me the head of John the Baptist here on a platter." [9] The king was grieved, yet out of regard for his oaths and for the guests, he commanded it to be given; [10] he sent and had John beheaded in the prison. [11] The head was brought on a platter and given to the girl, who brought it to her mother. [12] His disciples came and took the body and buried it; then they went and told Jesus.

[13] Now when Jesus heard this, he withdrew from there in a boat to a deserted place by himself. But when the crowds heard it, they followed him on foot from the towns. [14] When he went ashore, he saw a great crowd; and he had compassion for them and cured their sick. [15] When it was evening, the disciples came to him and said, "This is a deserted place, and the hour is now late; send the crowds away so that they may go into the villages and buy food for themselves." [16] Jesus said to them, "They need not go away; you give them something to eat." [17] They replied, "We have nothing here but five loaves and two fish." [18] And he said, "Bring them here to me." [19] Then he ordered the crowds to sit down on the grass. Taking the five loaves and the two fish, he looked up to heaven, and blessed and broke the loaves, and gave them to the disciples, and the disciples gave them to the crowds. [20] And all ate and were filled; and they took up what was left over of the broken pieces, twelve baskets full. [21] And those who ate were about five thousand men, besides women and children.

MATTHEW 14:1-21

2. **Based on Matthew 14:13, describe Jesus' response to John the Baptist's beheading. Beyond the text, what do you imagine Jesus was feeling after hearing of his cousin's death?**

Before we meditate on the first feeding-of-the-multitude story, a section of Scripture celebrating the provision of God, we have to pay attention to the immediate context of the story: the bloody, terrifying, and politically charged beheading of John the Baptist, Jesus' cousin. What an ominous start. Yes, Jesus' ministry was thriving. He was preaching that the Kingdom of God was near; he was healing droves of people through his gracious miracles. And yes, the disciples were growing in faith and in their commitment to Christ. But in the backdrop was a growing conflict between Jesus and the contemporary religious and governing leaders.

Rome was not pleased that Jesus was disrupting the "peace." The Jewish leaders were concerned that their people were falling away from the truth and into the guiles of a renegade miracle worker claiming to be the Jewish Messiah. But none of this opposition stopped Jesus from boldly preaching the gospel or quieted John the Baptist's testimony to Jesus' kingship. Together, Jesus and John the Baptist were making waves. So much so that when Herod killed John the Baptist it became a clear message to anyone following Jesus and the way of Jesus: *Conform to the way of the empire or your life might be at risk.*

Interestingly, it seems that King Herod regretted ordering John's death sentence but had no choice if he wanted to protect his own political power. Before John's disciples brought Jesus the news of John's tragic death, they buried John's mutilated body. Based on what is recorded in Scripture, Jesus didn't get to say goodbye to his cousin.

That's why I believe Jesus was eager to withdraw from the public side of his ministry. I think he was distraught over the death of his family member and ministry partner. Jesus experienced an all-too-common reality that Christians face in life: serving others while we are still grieving something ourselves. Despite his need to grieve and his desire to escape, the crowds found Jesus. How did he respond? He offered compassion to others when he needed comfort himself.

3. **Write out Matthew 14:14 below:**

4. **Describe a time you needed to be comforted by God but still had to find the capacity to have compassion for others. How did that season of ministry challenge your faith?**

5. **If you need God's comfort right now, write out a prayer to the Lord below:**

6. **Read Matthew 15:29-39. Underline everything Jesus says.**

29 After Jesus had left that place, he passed along the Sea of Galilee, and he went up the mountain, where he sat down. 30 Great crowds came to him, bringing with them the lame, the maimed, the blind, the mute, and many others. They put them at his feet, and he cured them, 31 so that the crowd was amazed when they saw the mute speaking, the maimed whole, the lame walking, and the blind seeing. And they praised the God of Israel.

[32] Then Jesus called his disciples to him and said, "I have compassion for the crowd, because they have been with me now for three days and have nothing to eat; and I do not want to send them away hungry, for they might faint on the way." [33] The disciples said to him, "Where are we to get enough bread in the desert to feed so great a crowd?" [34] Jesus asked them, "How many loaves have you?" They said, "Seven, and a few small fish." [35] Then ordering the crowd to sit down on the ground, [36] he took the seven loaves and the fish; and after giving thanks he broke them and gave them to the disciples, and the disciples gave them to the crowds. [37] And all of them ate and were filled; and they took up the broken pieces left over, seven baskets full. [38] Those who had eaten were four thousand men, besides women and children. [39] After sending away the crowds, he got into the boat and went to the region of Magadan.

MATTHEW 15:29-39

7. Use Matthew 14:1-21 and Matthew 15:29-39 to fill in the blanks.

COMPARING THE FEEDING-OF-THE-MULTITUDE STORIES

Matthew 14	Matthew 15
Jesus fed __________ men plus women and children.	Jesus fed __________ men plus women and children.
Deserted place—it was getting late, and the people were hungry.	Desolate place—there was nothing nearby to send the people to.
Jesus "had _____________ for them and cured their sick" (Matthew 14:14).	Jesus had "_____________ for the crowd" (Matthew 15:32).
Resources: ____ loaves ____ fish	Resources: ____ loaves ____ fish
Leftovers: ____ baskets	Leftovers: ____ baskets

8. List any reflections coming to your mind as you compare the two feeding-of-the-multitude stories.

9. Write out Matthew 15:32 below:

10. How does Jesus' consistent compassion encourage you?

As I meditate on these two stories, I can't help but wonder what it would have been like to be one of Jesus' disciples during these undeniable displays of his generosity and kindness. I find it interesting, and very convicting, that after Jesus healed the multitudes, the disciples did not ask Jesus to feed them as well. Maybe the disciples were trying to protect Jesus. After all, he had just lived through the earth-shattering loss of someone he loved. Or maybe they hoped to help Jesus preserve his energy. Maybe they were tired themselves and feeling compassion fatigue. Or perhaps they decided that Jesus had done enough for these needy people and it was time for them to be self-sufficient.

Whatever the case, I'm convinced that these stories were preserved for the original audience, and for you and me, so that we would appreciate and expect Jesus' abundance in our own lives. We need to relearn the ways of Jesus to rewire our natural tendency to expect little from God. *He's done enough on the cross,* we may think. We don't want to make him have to do more. But maybe that is the secondary point to these sections of Scripture: God *wants* to give us more of what we need.

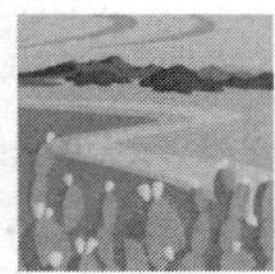

PART 3

UNDERSTANDING

Now that we've finished a close reading of the Scriptures, we're going to spend some time on interpretation: doing our best to understand what God was saying to the original audience and what he's teaching us through the process. But to do so, we need to learn his ways and consider how God's Word would have been understood by the original audience before applying the same truths to our own lives. "Scripture interpretation" may sound a little stuffy, but understanding what God means to communicate to us in the Bible is crucial to enjoying a close relationship with Jesus. Part 3 will enable you to answer the question *What does it mean?*

1. **Reread Matthew 14:13–21. Circle every time these words are used in the story: *send, away, go, here.***

13 Now when Jesus heard this, he withdrew from there in a boat to a deserted place by himself. But when the crowds heard it, they followed him on foot from the towns. 14 When he went ashore, he saw a great crowd; and he had compassion for them and cured their sick. 15 When it was evening, the disciples came to him and said, "This is a deserted place, and the hour is now late; send the crowds away so that they may go into the villages and buy food for themselves." 16 Jesus said to them, "They need not go away; you give them something to eat." 17 They replied, "We have nothing here but five loaves and two fish." 18 And he said, "Bring them here

to me." [19] Then he ordered the crowds to sit down on the grass. Taking the five loaves and the two fish, he looked up to heaven, and blessed and broke the loaves, and gave them to the disciples, and the disciples gave them to the crowds. [20] And all ate and were filled; and they took up what was left over of the broken pieces, twelve baskets full. [21] And those who ate were about five thousand men, besides women and children.

MATTHEW 14:13-21

2. **Reread Matthew 15:29-39. Circle every time these phrases are used in the story:** *at his feet, to him, send them away.*

[29] After Jesus had left [the district of Tyre and Sidon], he passed along the Sea of Galilee, and he went up the mountain, where he sat down. [30] Great crowds came to him, bringing with them the lame, the maimed, the blind, the mute, and many others. They put them at his feet, and he cured them, [31] so that the crowd was amazed when they saw the mute speaking, the maimed whole, the lame walking, and the blind seeing. And they praised the God of Israel.

[32] Then Jesus called his disciples to him and said, "I have compassion for the crowd, because they have been with me now for three days and have nothing to eat; and I do not want to send them away hungry, for they might faint on the way." [33] The disciples said to him, "Where are we to get enough bread in the desert to feed so great a crowd?" [34] Jesus asked them, "How many loaves have you?" They said, "Seven, and a few small fish." [35] Then ordering the crowd to sit down on the ground, [36] he took the seven loaves and the fish; and after giving thanks he broke them and gave them to the disciples, and the disciples gave them to the crowds. [37] And all of them ate and were filled; and they took up the broken pieces left over, seven baskets full. [38] Those who had eaten were four thousand men, besides women and children. [39] After sending away the crowds, he got into the boat and went to the region of Magadan.

MATTHEW 15:29-39

3. **Based on what you've just read, fill in the blanks.**

HOW THE DISCIPLES RESPONDED WHEN THE CROWDS WERE HUNGRY

Scripture	Multitudes	Problem	Disciples'/Jesus' Solution
Matthew 14	five thousand men plus women and children	Deserted place—it was getting late, and the people were hungry.	The disciples said, "Send the crowds ___________" (Matthew 14:15).
Matthew 15	four thousand men plus women and children	Desolate place—there was nothing nearby to send the people to.	Jesus said, "I do not want to send them ___________ hungry" (Matthew 15:32).

4. **How would these two experiences give the disciples perspective after Jesus' crucifixion, resurrection, and ascension?**

5. **How do you think the Jewish people witnessing these miracles reacted as Christ was talking and multiplying?**

Implied in both stories is Jesus' desire for the disciples to ask him to multiply the fish and loaves to feed the hungry masses. But they didn't ask Jesus to do more for the crowds; they tried to find a solution that involved sending the crowd away from Jesus.

This is a lesson for those of us feeling as if we don't have enough time, resources, or skills to meet the needs of our jobs and loved ones. I bet many of us are doing our best, maybe even exhausting ourselves with effort, to stay afloat in a culture that promotes busyness as a badge of honor and celebrates hustle as a natural part of making things happen. The pace and pressure of life seem determined to rob us of margin and consume us to the point of burnout.

In sharp contrast, Jesus invites us to approach him in our shortage, to ask him to meet all our needs in abundance, and to trust him when we are facing inadequacy and maybe even poverty of spirit or resources. He longs to go to great lengths on your behalf if you would but ask him for more. Why is it that we assume there is a limit to his compassion, his patience, his love? You can ask him for more. It is not selfish to bring your needs and wants to Christ.

6. **What do you need more of in your faith and life? Check all that apply and list any more you can think of.**

- ☐ faithfulness
- ☐ generosity
- ☐ gentleness
- ☐ hope
- ☐ joy
- ☐ kindness
- ☐ love
- ☐ money
- ☐ patience
- ☐ peace
- ☐ relationships
- ☐ self-control
- ☐ skills
- ☐ time
- ☐ work
- ☐ ______________________
- ☐ ______________________
- ☐ ______________________
- ☐ ______________________

7. **What have you tried on your own to make these resources stretch? What's working? What's not working?**

8. **If you were to bring your needs and your resources to God in prayer, what would you say? How would you ask Jesus to multiply what you have? Take the time to do that below.**

Jesus says some profound things to the disciples in these two desert events. Take a moment to write your name into these statements from Christ. Then pause long enough to absorb God's message to you in this moment.

+ Matthew 14:16 paraphrase: "You need not go away, _____________."

+ Matthew 15:32a paraphrase: "I have compassion for you, _____________."

+ Matthew 15:32b paraphrase: "I do not want to send you away hungry, _____________."

+ Matthew 15:34 paraphrase: "How many loaves have you, _____________?"

What if God is inviting us to ask him for more? Journaling this statement from Christ to me brought me to my knees: *Ask me for more, Kat.* You might be in a deserted or desolate place in life, somewhere that feels like an emotional or monetary desert, but remember, you're not there without a source of provision. Christ is with you now. And you can ask him for more of what you need. Dare we be people of God who believe he will provide us with what we need?

The brilliant Drs. Jeannine K. Brown and Kyle Roberts wrote my favorite commentary on Matthew, and in it they say this about the two feeding-of-the-multitude stories: "The two accounts share several details, and both echo the story of Moses providing food for Israel in their wilderness wanderings."[1] Here's a chart from Drs. Brown and Robert's commentary.[2]

OLD TESTAMENT ECHOES IN THE FEEDINGS OF THE MULTITUDES

Feeding of Five Thousand (Matthew 14:15–21)	Feeding of Four Thousand (15:32–39)	Echoing of OT Story
In a "deserted" (ἔρημος, *erēmos*) place (Matthew 14:15)	In a "deserted place" (ἐρημία, *erēmia*) (Matthew 15:33)	In the "desert" (ἔρημος, *erēmos*; Exodus 16:1, 3 LXX) of Sin
People have no food (Matthew 14:15)	People have no food (Matthew 15:32)	People have no food (Exodus 16:3)
Five loaves and two fish (Matthew 14:17)	Seven loaves and a few fish (Matthew 15:34)	Manna and quail provided (Exodus 16:13–14)
All ate and were full (Matthew 14:20)	All ate and were full (Matthew 15:37)	All had what they needed (Exodus 16:18)

9. Read Exodus 16:1-18. Underline anything that highlights the Lord's compassion.

16 The whole congregation of the Israelites set out from Elim; and Israel came to the wilderness of Sin, which is between Elim and Sinai, on the fifteenth day of the second month after they had departed from the land of Egypt. ² The whole congregation of the Israelites complained against Moses and Aaron in the wilderness. ³ The Israelites said to them, "If only we had died by the hand of the LORD in the land of Egypt, when we sat by the fleshpots and ate our fill of bread; for you have brought us out into this wilderness to kill this whole assembly with hunger."

⁴ Then the LORD said to Moses, "I am going to rain bread from heaven for you, and each day the people shall go out and gather enough for that day. In that way I will test them, whether they will follow my instruction or not. ⁵ On the sixth day, when they prepare what they bring in, it will be twice as much as they gather on other days." ⁶ So Moses and Aaron said to all the Israelites, "In the evening you shall know that it was the LORD who brought you out of the land of Egypt, ⁷ and in the morning you shall see the glory of the LORD, because he has heard your complaining against the LORD. For what are we, that you complain against us?" ⁸ And Moses said, "When the LORD gives you meat to eat in the evening and your fill of bread in the morning, because the LORD has heard the complaining that you utter against him—what are we? Your complaining is not against us but against the LORD."

⁹ Then Moses said to Aaron, "Say to the whole congregation of the Israelites, 'Draw near to the LORD, for he has heard your complaining.'" ¹⁰ And as Aaron spoke to the whole congregation of the Israelites, they looked toward the wilderness, and the glory of the LORD appeared in the cloud. ¹¹ The LORD spoke to Moses and said, ¹² "I have heard the complaining of the Israelites; say to them, 'At twilight you shall eat meat, and in the morning you shall have your fill of bread; then you shall know that I am the LORD your God.'"

[13] In the evening quails came up and covered the camp; and in the morning there was a layer of dew around the camp. [14] When the layer of dew lifted, there on the surface of the wilderness was a fine flaky substance, as fine as frost on the ground. [15] When the Israelites saw it, they said to one another, "What is it?" For they did not know what it was. Moses said to them, "It is the bread that the Lord has given you to eat. [16] This is what the Lord has commanded: 'Gather as much of it as each of you needs, an omer to a person according to the number of persons, all providing for those in their own tents.'" [17] The Israelites did so, some gathering more, some less. [18] But when they measured it with an omer, those who gathered much had nothing over, and those who gathered little had no shortage; they gathered as much as each of them needed.

EXODUS 16:1-18

10. What did the Israelites wish for in the desert?

11. In what ways has God's compassion been most evident in your life?

12. Where in your life and story do you need to experience more compassion from God?

✦ ✦ ✦

Let's check back in on our Deserts Storyline.

THE DESERTS STORYLINE OF SCRIPTURE

Location	Words from God for Desert Seasons	On the Other Side of the Desert
The Deserts of Shur and Beersheba (Genesis 16, 21)	[The angel of the LORD said,] "Where have you come from and where are you going?" (Genesis 16:8) [The angel of God said,] "What troubles you?" (Genesis 21:17)	Hagar went through rejection to get to protection.
The Desert of Dothan (Genesis 37, 45, 50)	[Joseph said,] "Do not be afraid! Am I in the place of God? Even though you intended to do harm to me, God intended it for good." (Genesis 50:19-20)	Joseph's brothers went through resentment to get to forgiveness.
The Desert of Sinai (Numbers 11, 14)	[The LORD said,] "How long will this people despise me? And how long will they refuse to believe in me, in spite of all the signs that I have done among them?" (Numbers 14:11)	The Israelites went through insecurity to get to belonging.
The Desert of Judea (Matthew 3–4)	[Jesus said,] "It is written, 'Do not put the Lord your God to the test.'" (Matthew 4:7)	Jesus went through trials to get to ministry.
The Deserts of Ministry (Matthew 14, 15)	[Jesus asked,] "How many loaves have you?" (Matthew 15:34)	The disciples went through scarcity to get to abundance.

1. What about the two feeding-of-the-multitude stories resonates with you most? What part of these stories piques your curiosity?

2. What did you learn about God in this lesson? And what did you learn about yourself in this lesson?

3. How should these truths shape your faith community and change you?

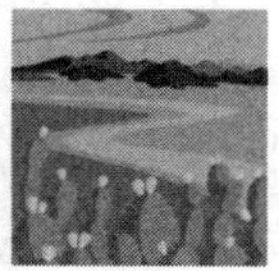

RESPONDING

The purpose of Bible study is to help you become more Christlike; that's why part 4 will include journaling space for your reflection on and responses to the content and a blank checklist for actionable next steps. You'll be able to process what you're learning so that you can live out the concepts and pursue Christlikeness. Part 4 will enable you to answer the questions *What truths is this passage teaching?* and *How do I apply this to my life?*

AT HIS LOWEST POINT, my husband showed me what it means to move through scarcity to enjoy God's abundance. It was fall of 2020, and the world was crawling out of its skin midpandemic. As if the global crises were not terrifying and isolating enough, polarizing political differences in the United States were fracturing our nation. Pastors like my husband found themselves ministering in a whole new world.

Aaron is seminary trained with twenty years of vocational pastoral leadership experience, and his training prepared him to equip a local church community through service, pastoral care, and theological study. He wasn't trained to be an epidemiologist, a medical professional, an economist, an educator, or a political analyst. Like many other ministers who were shepherding others during unprecedented times, Aaron was depleted.

When I feared he would buckle under the pressure, I witnessed him come to

God honestly, with nothing but overwhelming needs, so that he could receive from the Lord—asking not only for what he and our family needed from Christ but also that God would multiply his compassion for others. He could have crawled into bed and thrown the covers over his head, but instead, he admitted his weakness to meet the moment and turned to the One who is always crisis ready.

Aaron believes that the work of a pastor is not only to serve in a way that meets the needs of others but also to bring people to Jesus, who can meet all our needs. Aaron knows that Jesus multiplies. And that's just what happened in our local community. Yes, there were intense struggles, and we wouldn't wish that season on anyone. But through the scarcity, Aaron's faith was multiplied, and so was mine. Maybe that's the power of multiplication so easily missed when we experience depletion and lack: As God provides for one person, everyone else watching receives too—encouragement, hope, the faith of a mustard seed.

I wonder what desert you're in right now. Do you know how intensely Jesus cares about your needs? As we wrap up this final lesson, I want to share with you the ways the Lord challenged and encouraged me through the two feeding-of-the-multitude stories in deserted places.

1. COME TO JESUS WITH YOUR NEEDS.

To anyone who feels guilty asking Jesus for more, this one's for you. Yes, Jesus gave you his own life on the cross and then blessed you with undeserved grace. It almost feels wrong to expect more from God—he's already given too much. But your needs are not a burden to Christ. *You* are not a burden to Christ. It is God's joy to give you good gifts. That's why Jesus says to come to him even when we are weary—because he wants to give us the rest we need. And so I'll challenge you to come to Jesus with your needs. Resist the urge to qualify your prayers with *I hate to ask this of you* or *If it wouldn't cause too much trouble* or *If you get to everyone else whose needs are greater than my own.* Boldly, desperately approach Christ in prayer and honestly confess what you need. I'm concerned that some of us are not approaching Christ unreservedly because we think he's going to be put out by our requests, distracted from the "more important" work he's got going on taking care of the rest of the world. Or that he's annoyed by interruptions. Beloved, he wouldn't exhort us to pray without ceasing (1 Thessalonians 5:17) if he couldn't handle our requests. Take him at his word. Come to Jesus in your desert.

2. BRING WHAT LITTLE YOU HAVE TO JESUS.

It has been my experience that I want to "be prepared" to bring my needs to Jesus, kind of how I like to tidy up my house before the housekeeper comes to do the real cleaning. I sometimes think of Jesus as someone who needs or would appreciate my help. Additionally, I prefer to come to Jesus when I have a lot to show for my efforts. *Jesus, I'm going to ask you for a big thing now because I just finished writing a Bible-study lesson. Jesus, this request is a real doozy, but remember, I spent time reading the Bible this week.* Why is it that I resist approaching Christ in prayer with meager offerings? The plain and simple thing is that I don't like thinking of bringing just a few fish and a few loaves to Jesus when I request his help. I like to bring a résumé. We don't need to bring a lot to Jesus; we just need to bring what we have. And if what we have is very little, so be it. That's why we are coming to Christ in the first place.

3. ACCEPT JESUS' MINISTRY OF MULTIPLICATION.

I tend to curb my joy to protect myself from disappointment—as if that is any way to enjoy living. I used to try not to place expectations on God because I didn't want to be disappointed when he didn't seem to answer my prayers. You know what happened to my prayer life? It stopped. I had no reason to ask Jesus to meet my needs without admitting I had real needs and believing he could meet them. By the time I was ready to surrender to Christ and admit my needs, my new challenge became accepting his help. I wanted God to help me just enough to get me through and then leave the rest to me or others. *Give me a little leg up, Lord, and I'll lift myself the rest of the way. Give me no more than I imagine is possible, something measurable and modest that will work.* Now I'm learning a new way to pray and bring my needs to Jesus. I'm practicing expecting God's best and enjoying when he does immeasurably more than I ask for or imagine. But it hasn't come naturally to me. Whether this is your struggle or not, I bet all of us need to be challenged by the Holy Spirit to receive the abundance Christ offers us through his ministry of multiplication. Let's accept it.

Use this journaling space to process what you are learning.

Ask yourself how these truths impact your relationship with God and with others.

What is the Holy Spirit bringing to your mind as actionable next steps in your faith journey?

+

+

+

As You Go

THE DESERTLIKE SEASONS of our lives are lonely, scary places. If not for God's staying presence and faithful provision, we might be tempted to give up hope when we wander in our wildernesses. Instead, you and I have a radically different option available to us: We can view each desert as a way forward in our journeys so that we can later arrive more connected to Christ than before. God is leading you through something to get you to goodness on the other side.

I've been praying wholeheartedly for you. That you would finish the study; that you would get to this page and believe with your whole heart, soul, mind, and strength that Jesus is with you in your desert. He is your wise guide and faithful companion. He is your ever-present help in time of need. And he can't wait to meet your needs and multiply the blessings in your life.

+ If God was able to lead Hagar through the Deserts of Shur and Beersheba, he can lead you through rejection to protection.

+ If God was able to lead Joseph through the Desert of Dothan, he can lead you through resentment to restoration.

+ If God was able to lead Moses and the Israelites through their wilderness wanderings in the Desert of Sinai, he can lead you through insecurity to belonging.

+ If God was able to lead Jesus through his test in the Desert of Judea, he can lead you through trials to ministry opportunities.

+ If God was able to lead Jesus' disciples through the Deserts of Ministry, where Jesus fed thousands of hungry people, he can lead you through scarcity to abundance.

Believe it.

PS: I've loved this time with you, and I hope you join me again for another journey in the **Storyline Bible Studies**.

THE DESERTS STORYLINE OF SCRIPTURE

Location	Words from God for Desert Seasons	On the Other Side of the Desert
The Deserts of Shur and Beersheba (Genesis 16, 21)	[The angel of the LORD said,] "Where have you come from and where are you going?" (Genesis 16:8) [The angel of God said,] "What troubles you?" (Genesis 21:17)	Hagar went through rejection to get to protection.
The Desert of Dothan (Genesis 37, 45, 50)	[Joseph said,] "Do not be afraid! Am I in the place of God? Even though you intended to do harm to me, God intended it for good." (Genesis 50:19-20)	Joseph's brothers went through resentment to get to forgiveness.
The Desert of Sinai (Numbers 11, 14)	[The LORD said,] "How long will this people despise me? And how long will they refuse to believe in me, in spite of all the signs that I have done among them?" (Numbers 14:11)	The Israelites went through insecurity to get to belonging.
The Desert of Judea (Matthew 3–4)	[Jesus said,] "It is written, 'Do not put the Lord your God to the test.'" (Matthew 4:7)	Jesus went through trials to get to ministry.
The Deserts of Ministry (Matthew 14, 15)	[Jesus asked,] "How many loaves have you?" (Matthew 15:34)	The disciples went through scarcity to get to abundance.

Each **Storyline Bible Study** is five lessons long and can be paired with its thematic partner for a seamless ten-week study. Complement the *Deserts* study with

GARDENS
GROWING AN EVERGREEN FAITH
IN A TRUSTWORTHY GOD

The *Gardens* Bible study will guide you through five Scripture passages set in gardens. The presence of this setting is a key element in each one, revealing something about God—and about us.

Learn more at thestorylineproject.com.

CP2059

Storyline Bible Studies

Each study follows people, places, or things throughout the Bible.
This approach allows you to see the cohesive storyline of Scripture
and appreciate the Bible as the literary masterpiece that it is.

**Access free resources to help you teach or
lead a small group at thestorylineproject.com.**

CP1816

Acknowledgments

WITHOUT MY FAMILY'S SUPPORT, the **Storyline Bible Studies** would just be a dream. I'm exceedingly grateful for a family that prays and cheers for me when I step out to try something new. To my husband, Aaron; son, Caleb; and mom, Noemi: You three sacrificed the most to ensure that I had enough time and space to write. Thank you. And to all my extended family: I know an army of Armstrongs was praying and my family in Austin was cheering me on to the finish line. Thank you.

NavPress and Tyndale teams: Thank you for believing in me. You wholeheartedly embraced the concept, and you've made this project better in every way possible. Special thanks to David Zimmerman, my amazing editor Caitlyn Carlson, Elizabeth Schroll, Olivia Eldredge, David Geeslin, and the entire editorial and marketing teams.

All my friends rallied to pray for this project when I was stressed about the deadlines. Thank you. We did it! Without your intercession, these wouldn't be complete. I want to give special thanks to my closest friends and my Tuesday night Bible-study group: Ashley W. and G., Abby, Amy, Ellen, Hanah, Kylie, Laura L. and V., Lauren, Leigh, Lisa, Regina, Sami, Sarah, Sydney, and Tabitha.

Resources for Deeper Study

OLD TESTAMENT

The Africana Bible: Reading Israel's Scriptures from Africa and the African Diaspora, ed. Hugh R. Page Jr.

And God Spoke to Abraham: Preaching from the Old Testament by Fleming Rutledge

Bearing God's Name: Why Sinai Still Matters by Carmen Joy Imes

The Epic of Eden: A Christian Entry into the Old Testament by Sandra L. Richter

The IVP Bible Background Commentary: Old Testament by John H. Walton, Victor H. Matthews, and Mark W. Chavalas

The Lost World of Genesis One: Ancient Cosmology and the Origins Debate by John H. Walton

Opening Israel's Scriptures by Ellen F. Davis

The Pentateuch as Narrative: A Biblical-Theological Commentary, Library of Biblical Interpretation, by John H. Sailhamer

The Universal Story: Genesis 1–11, Transformative Word Series, by Dru Johnson

NEW TESTAMENT
Echoes of Scripture in the Gospels by Richard B. Hays

The Gospel according to Matthew, New Collegeville Bible Commentary, by Barbara E. Reid

The Gospels as Stories: A Narrative Approach to Matthew, Mark, Luke, and John by Jeannine K. Brown

An Introduction to the New Testament, 2nd ed., by D. A. Carson and Douglas J. Moo

The Jewish Annotated New Testament: New Revised Standard Version Bible Translation, 2nd ed., eds. Amy-Jill Levine and Marc Zvi Brettler

John: A Commentary, The New Testament Library, by Marianne Meye Thompson

John's Wisdom: A Commentary on the Fourth Gospel by Ben Witherington III

Matthew, The Two Horizons New Testament Commentary, by Jeannine K. Brown and Kyle Roberts

The New Testament in Its World: An Introduction to the History, Literature, and Theology of the First Christians by N. T. Wright and Michael F. Bird

True to Our Native Land: An African American New Testament Commentary, ed. Brian K. Blount

BIBLE STUDY
Commentary on the New Testament Use of the Old Testament, eds. G. K. Beale and D. A. Carson

Dictionary of Biblical Imagery, eds. Leland Ryken, James C. Wilhoit, and Tremper Longman III

The Drama of Scripture: Finding Our Place in the Biblical Story by Craig G. Bartholomew and Michael W. Goheen

From Beginning to Forever: A Study of the Grand Narrative of Scripture by Elizabeth Woodson

How (Not) to Read the Bible: Making Sense of the Anti-Women, Anti-Science, Pro-Violence, Pro-Slavery and Other Crazy-Sounding Parts of Scripture by Dan Kimball

How to Read the Bible as Literature . . . and Get More out of It by Leland Ryken

Literarily: How Understanding Bible Genres Transforms Bible Study by Kristie Anyabwile

The Mission of God: Unlocking the Bible's Grand Narrative by Christopher J. H. Wright

"Reading Scripture as a Coherent Story" by Richard Bauckham, in *The Art of Reading Scripture*, eds. Ellen F. Davis and Richard B. Hays

Reading While Black: African American Biblical Interpretation as an Exercise in Hope by Esau McCaulley

Read the Bible for a Change: Understanding and Responding to God's Word by Ray Lubeck

Scripture as Communication: Introducing Biblical Hermeneutics by Jeannine K. Brown

South Asia Bible Commentary: A One-Volume Commentary on the Whole Bible, ed. Brian Wintle

Theological Bible Commentary, eds. Gail R. O'Day and David L. Petersen

Vindicating the Vixens: Revisiting Sexualized, Vilified, and Marginalized Women of the Bible, ed. Sandra Glahn

What Is the Bible and How Do We Understand It? by Dennis R. Edwards

Women's Bible Commentary, 3rd ed., eds. Carol A. Newsom, Sharon H. Ringe, and Jacqueline E. Lapsley

Words of Delight: A Literary Introduction to the Bible by Leland Ryken

About the Author

KAT ARMSTRONG was born in Houston, Texas, where the humidity ruins her Mexi-German curls. She is a powerful voice in our generation as a sought-after Bible teacher, preacher, and leader, and she's on a mission to spark holy curiosity in a generation of Bible readers. She holds a master's degree from Dallas Theological Seminary and is pursuing a doctorate of ministry in New Testament context. Kat is the author of *No More Holding Back*, *The In-Between Place*, and the **Storyline Bible Studies**. She is the cofounder of the Polished Network and the host of the *Holy Curiosity* podcast. She and her husband, Aaron, have been married for over twenty years; live in McKinney, Texas, with their son, Caleb; and attend the church in McKinney where Aaron serves as the lead pastor.

KATARMSTRONG.COM

@KATARMSTRONG1

THESTORYLINEPROJECT.COM

@THESTORYLINEPROJECT

Make peace with your past.
Find hope in the present.
Step into your future.

Available everywhere books are sold.

Notes

LESSON ONE | GOING THROUGH REJECTION TO GET TO PROTECTION

1. Tremper Longman III and Raymond B. Dillard, *An Introduction to the Old Testament*, 2nd ed. (Grand Rapids: Zondervan Academic, 2006), 70.
2. John H. Walton, Victor H. Matthews, and Mark W. Chavalas, *The IVP Bible Background Commentary: Old Testament* (Downers Grove, IL: InterVarsity Press, 2000), 48.
3. Walton, Matthews, and Chavalas, *IVP Bible Background Commentary*, 48.
4. Walton, Matthews, and Chavalas, *IVP Bible Background Commentary*, 48.
5. Walton, Matthews, and Chavalas, *IVP Bible Background Commentary*, 49.
6. Walton, Matthews, and Chavalas, *IVP Bible Background Commentary*, 43.
7. Walton, Matthews, and Chavalas, *IVP Bible Background Commentary*, 43.
8. Susan Niditch, "Genesis," in *Women's Bible Commentary*, 3rd ed., ed. Carol A. Newsom, Sharon H. Ringe, and Jacqueline E. Lapsley (Louisville: Westminster John Knox Press, 2012), 36.

LESSON TWO | GOING THROUGH RESENTMENT TO GET TO FORGIVENESS

1. *Avengers: Endgame* (Burbank, CA: Marvel Studios, 2019), DVD.
2. Leland Ryken, *Words of Delight: A Literary Introduction to the Bible*, 2nd ed. (Grand Rapids: Baker Academic, 1992), 101.
3. Theodore Hiebert, "Genesis," in *Theological Bible Commentary*, ed. Gail R. O'Day and David L. Petersen (Louisville: Westminster John Knox Press, 2009), 23.
4. Leland Ryken, James C. Wilhoit, and Tremper Longman III, eds. *Dictionary of Biblical Imagery* (Downers Grove, IL: InterVarsity Press, 1998), 948–51.
5. Ryken, *Words of Delight*, 100.

LESSON THREE | GOING THROUGH INSECURITY TO GET TO BELONGING

1. Carmen Joy Imes, *Bearing God's Name: Why Sinai Still Matters* (Downers Grove, IL: InterVarsity Press, 2019), 105.
2. Fleming Rutledge, *And God Spoke to Abraham: Preaching from the Old Testament* (Grand Rapids: Eerdmans, 2011), 90.

LESSON FOUR | GOING THROUGH TRIALS TO GET TO MINISTRY

1. Kat Armstrong, "Ever Traced the Links between Jesus & Moses? 5 Surprising Commonalities," Logos, December 19, 2023, https://www.logos.com/grow/nook-jesus-and-moses.
2. Armstrong, "Ever Traced the Links?"
3. David Seal, "Son of God," in *The Lexham Bible Dictionary*, ed. John D. Barry (Bellingham, WA: Lexham Press, 2016).

LESSON FIVE | GOING THROUGH SCARCITY TO GET TO ABUNDANCE

1. Jeannine K. Brown and Kyle Roberts, *Matthew*, The Two Horizons New Testament Commentary (Grand Rapids: Eerdmans, 2018), 139.
2. Brown and Roberts, *Matthew*, 139. Chart included with permission from the copyright holder.